Fading Out of the JW Cult

A Memoir

Fading Out of the JW Cult

A Memoir

Bonnie Zieman

Copyright © 2016 Bonnie Zieman
All rights reserved. No part of this book may be reproduced or transmitted in any form or by any means, without the written permission of the author.
ISBN: 1517270189
ISBN-13: 9781517270186
Library of Congress Control Number: 2015914931
CreateSpace Independent Publishing Platform
North Charleston, South Carolina

Dedication

To Rumi, 13th century poet, scholar and mystic whose ecumenical verse provided comfort and direction through the dark days and continues to inspire me now.

*"Why are you knocking at every other door?
Go, knock at the door of your own heart."*
~Rumi

Cover & Digital Design by Bonnie Zieman, Copyright © 2016
Cover photograph by Bonnie Zieman, Copyright © 2016
Photographs property of Bonnie Zieman, except where otherwise noted.

Table of Contents

Acknowledgments··· xi
Introduction··· xiii
Chapter 1 Prologue – An Overview······························· 1
Chapter 2 The Gift·· 5
Chapter 3 Beginnings Explain a Lot····························· 14
Chapter 4 Mom & Dad - For Better······························ 19
Chapter 5 Baby Breaks the Spell································· 28
Chapter 6 Early Indoctrination & Impressions················ 32
Chapter 7 Vancouver, British Columbia························ 35
Chapter 8 Accessory to a Crime·································· 40
Chapter 9 Mount Pleasant Congregation······················ 45
Chapter 10 The Hows··· 52
Chapter 11 But Please Mommy!···································· 55
Chapter 12 I Am ... Alive!··· 60
Chapter 13 Book Study Conductor································ 62
Chapter 14 A False Self··· 66
Chapter 15 Excluding Myself·· 71
Chapter 16 The Principal's Office·································· 76
Chapter 17 Working Girls & JW Creeps··························· 81
Chapter 18 Conditional Acceptance······························ 89
Chapter 19 The Slap··· 92
Chapter 20 One Rejection Too Many······························ 96
Chapter 21 Ambitions··· 102

Chapter 22	Collateral Damage	107
Chapter 23	Love & Marriage	114
Chapter 24	Special Pioneering	122
Chapter 25	Undue Influence & Acting Out	126
Chapter 26	Gentlemen Prefer Blondes	135
Chapter 27	The Need is Great	139
Chapter 28	Manipulation & Exploitation	141
Chapter 29	Are You Happy?	148
Chapter 30	Circuit Work or Baby?	151
Chapter 31	How Much More?	157
Chapter 32	Fred Franz	160
Chapter 33	Let Us Entertain You	164
Chapter 34	Horny? ... Who Me?	168
Chapter 35	Options & Decisions	171
Chapter 36	'Corporate' Espionage	177
Chapter 37	Life – OUT	183
Chapter 38	You're Kidding ... Right?	189
Chapter 39	Hey Mom ... Over Here	193
Chapter 40	Millions Now Loyal, Will Also Die	200
	Epilogue	205
	Recommended Reading	213
	About the Author	219

Acknowledgments

Thank you to my loved ones for gracing my life with your amazing presence, and for providing the inspiration and support essential to the writing of these emotion-resurrecting reflections.

Introduction

An Overview of History & Practices of Jehovah's Witnesses (for those not yet familiar with the group):

Jehovah's Witnesses grew out of the "*Bible Students*" movement founded in the latter part of the 19th century by Charles Taze Russell. In 1931, under the leadership of Joseph F. Rutherford, the name "*Jehovah's Witnesses*" was formally adopted by the movement.

As of 2015 Jehovah's Witnesses have approximately 8,000,000 followers in more than 100,000 congregations around the planet. In 2001 The Watchtower Bible and Tract Society of New York was named among the top forty revenue-generating companies in New York City. Being incorporated as a religion, they pay no taxes on their millions (perhaps billions) in revenue and holdings. The Jehovah's Witness organization and its members are directed by a "Governing Body", a small group of male elders residing at the corporate headquarters presently in Brooklyn, New York. Over the years, they have created several not-for-profit corporate entities which oversee the diverse interests of the sect, some of which are:

- Watchtower Bible and Tract Society of Pennsylvania,
- Watchtower Bible and Tract Society of New York, Inc.,
- Religious Order of Jehovah's Witnesses, New York,
- Kingdom Support Services, Inc., New York,
- International Bible Students Association (IBSA) (United Kingdom)
- Watchtower Bible and Tract Society of Canada
- Watchtower Bible & Tract Society of Australia, Inc.

- Christian Congregation of Jehovah's Witnesses, Inc.,
- JW.ORG

Several of the above entities were formed in the year 2000 after a major reorganization in their corporate structure. Recent reorganizing and rebranding efforts have resulted in the creation of their new logo and website "JW.ORG", and their own JW broadcasting studio.

Current Watchtower Headquarters in Brooklyn, New York. Buildings in this mega-complex are being sold off, and new headquarters and plants are being built in Warwick, New York. (Image from en.wikipedia.org)

Only the Governing Body of Jehovah's Witnesses interprets the Bible, establishes doctrine, determines organizational policies and practices, oversees regulations about the appointment and responsibilities of elders, determines how judicial committees convened against accused sinners shall proceed, and decides upon all congregational procedures for its followers.

Jehovah's Witnesses have their own translation of the Bible, "*The New World Translation of The Holy Scriptures*". They write, publish and print millions of magazines, books and pamphlets in hundreds of languages. Adherents distribute the printed matter in the preaching work and through other multi-media methods. The WBTS owns printing plants to facilitate their publishing work across the globe. Workers in these facilities are mainly unpaid volunteers.

Jehovah's Witnesses are known as a fundamentalist, Bible-based sect relying on a literal translation of scripture (except for the most obvious poetic or symbolic passages). They posit that we are now living in "*the end times*", that Jehovah God's "*Battle of Armageddon*" is ever-imminent, at which time the wicked will be destroyed and God's faithful followers (Jehovah's Witnesses) will survive to live forever on a paradise Earth. They believe only 144,000 specially anointed humans will be resurrected to heavenly glory to reign as kings with Christ. Since the last members of this select group of 144,000 were said to have been chosen at the beginning of the twentieth century, the number still on Earth in this twenty-first century should be dwindling.

Jehovah's Witnesses are known for their proselytizing work, their refusal of blood transfusions and their political neutrality, which compels adherents to refuse to defend their country in the military, vote, salute the flag, or sing national anthems. JWs do not celebrate common holidays with the rest of society, believing most celebrations, such as Christmas, Easter and birthdays, etc. have pagan origins. Followers are told to keep separate from "*the world*" which is considered to be under the influence of Satan and, therefore, immoral and corrupt. Witnesses believe only they have the truth and refer to themselves as being "*in the truth*".

Any baptized member of Jehovah's Witnesses who engages in unscriptural, "*worldly*" activities or any baptized member no longer loyal to the Governing Body or JW organization undergo a requisite disciplinary action known as "*disfellowshipping*". (Disfellowshipping which is similar to excommunication, is being cast out of or banished from the congregation. Anyone so disciplined is considered to be among those who will be destroyed at the Battle of Armageddon).

Those still in "*good standing*" with the organization are instructed by the Governing Body to shun disassociated and disfellowshipped members. Witnesses shun anyone who speaks out against the organization and refer to them with the word "*apostate*". Reinstatement is possible only if one is truly repentant, recommits to a study of the Bible and the Watchtower publications, views the Governing Body as God's Earthly instrument and regularly attends the meetings.

Jehovah's Witnesses do not believe in the trinity, in hell, that the soul is immortal, and they reject the theory of evolution. They operate as a theocracy with a hierarchical arrangement descending from Jehovah God at the top, to Christ, to the Governing Body, to branch and circuit overseers, to the elders, to the "brothers", and at the bottom with no authority are women, who are required to be in submission to the elders and their husbands.

There have been recent news reports and governmental commissions across the globe, due to Jehovah's Witnesses persistent lack of reporting to proper authorities, the sexual abuse of minors by members of the congregation (including elders and ministerial servants). News reports document how many of the elders/ministerial servants accused of child sexual abuse have been allowed to keep (or later resume) their appointed positions in the congregation because it is only the accuser's word against the word of the accused. To take formal action against an accused abuser, JW.ORG requires *"two witnesses"* of the actual act of abuse.

The damaging effects (depression, mental disorders and suicide) experienced by defectors from the cult, due to the Jehovah's Witnesses' rigid practice of shunning are frequently reported. Legal cases are now pending against the Watchtower Bible & Tract Society due to interference in the lives of former members by this requirement of current members to shun them.

Typical Characteristics of a Cult

If you wonder why the title of this memoir names Jehovah's Witnesses as a cult instead of a religion, you need only consult the following list of common characteristics of a cult:

1. cults have authoritarian leadership
2. cults demand loyalty and submission to that leadership
3. cults say only they have the truth or know the way
4. cults control thinking and access to information
5. cults discourage independent, critical thinking
6. cult members are encouraged to be dependent
7. cults use members to work for no or little monetary remuneration

8. cults keep financial records and organizational procedures secret
9. cults are often apocalyptic or doomsday and believe only they will survive the end
10. cults make utopian promises about the future
11. cults offer instant community and fellowship
12. cults are often anti-family, anti-woman, anti-child
13. cults use a hierarchical organizational structure
14. cults use exclusive terminology and references
15. cults denigrate competing groups or organizations
16. cults teach that members are special and exempt
17. cults view questioning and doubting as disloyal
18. cults have a strong emphasis on recruitment
19. cults expect current members to recruit new members
20. cults claim only they can explain the world and the future
21. cult members believe they are working for greater good and not for the cult per se
22. cults control behaviours and activities of members with rigid schedules
23. cults often control grooming, dress, associations, education, etc.
24. cults cultivate an "*us/them*" mentality with regard to the world
25. cults prepare adepts to expect opposition or persecution from non-members ("*the world*")
26. cults claim special mission from God or universe
27. cults often re-write unsavoury details of their own history
28. cults emphasize the need for donations to continue their mission
29. cults are invasive and interfere in private lives of members
30. cults cultivate high levels of fear in members
31. cults induce guilt for lack of obedience or conformity
32. cults induce fears/phobias of leaving the group
33. cults isolate members and create fear of the outside world
34. cult members are promised special, future rewards for loyal service
35. cult leaders do not accept normal social responsibilities, feeling that because they are special, they are exempt
36. cult leaders do not assume responsibility for errors they commit within the group
37. cults use threats and intimidation to control members
38. cult thinking is invariably "*black/white*", "*either/or*"

39. cults work hard to protect their image and feel they have the right to mislead, if in the service of God, the greater good or the group
40. cult members must give up personal identity and goals
41. cult members must suspend disbelief
42. cult members seem to be unaware they are being controlled and will vigorously deny it
43. cult members are not only spiritually abused, but sometimes also physically, psychologically, emotionally and/or sexually abused
44. cult members become unable to make their own decisions without consulting an outside authority, the cult
45. cult members experience many double-bind situations
46. cults mete out punishments upon those who leave or wish to leave
47. cult members often feel trapped and that there is no dignified way to exit the group
48. cult members who speak against the group or its leaders are excommunicated and then punished with shunning
49. cults threaten death, immediate or future, symbolic or real, to members who decide to leave the group
50. cults are deceptive with information they offer to public, governments, and/or to the media. (The JW cult secretly refer to these deceptions as *"theocratic warfare"*, although they vigorously deny the use of this tactic.)

In view of the above fifty random characteristics of a cult, Jehovah's Witnesses can certainly be said to fall within the category of "cult" more than the category of "religion", as they claim for tax exemption purposes. In this memoir, I refer to Jehovah's Witnesses both as a cult and a sect and, on occasion, use their word "religion" when contextually appropriate. The above list was compiled with information from Michael Langone, Psychologist; Margaret Thaler Singer, Psychologist; Steven Hassan, Counselor; and other sociological and psychological information accumulated from personal and professional observation, experience and training.

"A ruling intelligentsia ... treats the masses as raw material to be experimented on, processed, and wasted at will." ~Eric Hoffer, The Temper of Our Time

"Cults can hide in many places. They are so adept at blending into society and masking their true colors that often their victims do not realize that they were even in a cult until they have escaped it. Nor do they fully comprehend the severity of the brainwashing that they were subjected to, until they are finally free of it." ~Natacha Tormey, Cults - A Bloodstained History

CHAPTER 1

Prologue – An Overview

After a long internal struggle I faded out of the Jehovah's Witness cult about the same time that Watchtower Governing Body member, Raymond Franz, had his *"Crisis of Conscience"*.

Raymond Franz, while doing research for publications he was writing for the Watchtower Society, discovered discrepancies in their beliefs, practices and prophecies. The other members of the Governing Body refused to address his legitimate concerns about these discrepancies. Ray Franz realized he could not remain affiliated with an organization that was not following, and even distorting, the Bible. He resigned from the Governing Body and left the New York headquarters. The remaining members of the Governing Body, desperate to discredit him and any information he might publicly disclose, soon found a flimsy excuse to excommunicate him. After a lifetime of loyal service to the Watchtower Society, Ray Franz and his wife found themselves with no home, no children, no income, no work prospects, no contacts and no pensions. Such dismissals of longtime, volunteer workers are not uncommon in the Watchtower organization and have left many upright, loyal servants destitute.

Other volunteers at the Watchtower headquarters, who expressed similar doubts at the same time as Raymond Franz, were also summarily dismissed and discarded. They may have been devoted servants for thirty or forty years, but share a concern, ask a question, express a doubt, and all those years of service counted for naught. The Watchtower Society demonstrated and continues to demonstrate no appropriate 'duty of care' to those who sacrifice personal goals and normal family lives to work for years in their offices or printing plants.

It was two decades after the Watchtower's breach of trust with regard to Raymond Franz that I finally became aware of the upheaval at the Brooklyn headquarters in the nineteen-eighties. Had I known about the crisis at Brooklyn Bethel and Raymond Franz's departure at that time, I might not have felt so alone in my efforts to leave the sect.

When I was struggling to leave, there were no Facebook groups or YouTube channels presenting documented evidence about Watchtower misdeeds by Witnesses who had already claimed their freedom. My husband served as an elder from the time I met him and, as the assembly servant for our circuit, he had many *"theocratic"* responsibilities. It took him a little longer, therefore, to extricate himself from their grip. While he did not dispute my backing away, he was confused and dismayed by my gradual exit process, and I was having trouble finding the courage to leave ... alone.

It really would have emboldened me to know a member of the Governing Body had also experienced enough doubts to leave. But all of that is water under the bridge. I did finally fade out in spite of my many fears and doubts. Getting out was one thing. Clearing away the vestiges of indoctrination, undue influence, grief for all the lost years, and then dealing with the imposed shunning by family and friends, was another.

Once totally *'inactive'*, feelings of freedom and relief were often mixed with guilt, loneliness and a profound sadness as a life ostracized from my family of origin loomed. I wish I had known then, what I know now about how to recover from having a life stolen and a mind co-opted. It would have been helpful to have known of ways to jump-start healing after escape from a high-control group and during the challenging re-entry and adaptation to normal life. (If you now find yourself in a similar position, you can find help in my book, "*Exiting the JW Cult:* **A Healing Handbook** *for Current & Former Jehovah's Witnesses*".)

But I am jumping ahead of myself. For now, in this overview, you need to know that I was born "*in the truth*", became a pioneer, a special pioneer and married an elder/presiding overseer. We pioneered and served where "*the need was great*" in French-speaking Quebec, Canada. Our young married life revolved totally around being special representatives of Jehovah's Witnesses. As it became clear to me that I could no longer continue as a member of the organization, it was difficult to imagine how to get out without blowing my whole life apart. It seemed the only way to preserve my marriage was to slowly fade my way out and hope my husband would eventually follow. This memoir will share what led to my wanting to leave and how the leaving actually unfolded.

It is my hope that by sharing some of my experiences, both in and out of the cult, that other Jehovah's Witnesses, at whatever point they find themselves in their awakening, will be helped. I intend to share the salient parts of my journey as a Jehovah's Witness - many good, many difficult, some bizarre, some amusing. The challenges faced after having exited will also be shared. Many things since learned as a student of psychology and as a psychotherapist will also be disclosed, that had I known back then, would have made my exit so much easier. The occasional clinical insights are added with the hope they will shine a light on the path for the many others on a similar odyssey.

The effects experienced from being raised in a high-control group are not unique to me. Anyone currently in a cult, in the process of exiting one, or in the process of recovering from having been in any high-control or abusive situation will have moments of recognition as they read these pages. It helps to read another person's first-hand account. Moments of recognition ("*That's just how I felt!*", "*That happened to me, too!*") help affirm that you are not alone and/or are not going crazy.

I never kept a journal of the events of my life as one of Jehovah's Witnesses or of the thoughts and feelings I experienced during that time. What appears here is shared from memory. While most of these memories were threshold moments in my life and, therefore, imprinted in my brain, it is well documented that memory can be unreliable and/or biased. There may be others who were present at particular events who recall them differently. It is a given that there will be variations in accounts of *any* experience. We experience our lives subjectively, not objectively. All one can do is be as authentic and truthful as individual human memory allows. None of the scenes or conversations in this memoir are invented or embellished for dramatic effect. They all happened and are all recorded on the page to the best of my ability.

Since I was either alarmed, amused, outraged, puzzled, embarrassed or traumatized by many of my experiences as a Jehovah's Witness, the memories are deeply imbedded and distinct. Recounting these experiences to friends and family over the years also kept them alive. However, conversations shared here cannot all be verbatim - though they did come quickly and easily to mind. I offer you my recollections, my perspective, my truth, my interpretations and my insights. That's all one can do and ultimately that *is* what constitutes *a memoir*.

Of course, my bias against, and antipathy for, JW.ORG as a coercive, repressive, quasi-religious group will be evident ... here and there. The title is *"Fading **OUT** of the JW Cult"* after all. A memoir with no position, no personal point of view, or no opinion would be flat, banal, wooden and hardly worth your time. Since my right to think, dream, choose and live freely was interfered with by JW.ORG, it stands to reason that the story of my association with the cult will be recounted with just a bit of personal bias. I make no apology for that. To eliminate all bias would not be an accurate representation of who I was, who I am now, and what I feel. However, this is not a book dedicated to exposing the crimes and misdemeanors of JW.ORG. It is simply a memoir of *my* thirty year association with them, what I learned about the organization during that time, how affiliation with them affected me, and how I finally set myself free. Knowing all I know about this organization and being keenly aware of my particular prejudices and leanings, I do make an effort to be fair ... here and there.

In order to respect privacy, only some names of people who played a part in my story of life as a Jehovah's Witness are revealed. It's my preference to create pseudonyms, use real or pseudo initials, or in some cases, leave the names out altogether. Where real names are used, it is so noted.

I begin inspired by the words of Persian poet and mystic, Jelaluddin Balkhi Rumi:

> *There is a candle in your heart,*
> *ready to be kindled.*
> *There is a void in your soul,*
> *ready to be filled.*
> *You feel it, don't you?*
> *~Rumi*

CHAPTER 2

The Gift

November 18, 1978 - Guyana: – *More than 900 people (300 of them children) die after drinking Flavor-Aid spiked with cyanide, under instructions from their cult leader Jim Jones. The massacre began with the murders of a California congressman and journalists who had gone to Jonestown, Guyana to investigate reports of abuse of the followers of the charismatic Jim Jones of the People's Temple.*

News stories, like the one paraphrased above, shocked the world in the autumn of 1978 and certainly rattled me. After listening to the many reports about the immensity of the tragedy, I remember consoling myself thinking *"Well, at least Jehovah's Witnesses are not led by such a self-serving, homicidal maniac. Witnesses may be weird, but at least we're not a cult like the People's Temple!"* The followers of Jim Jones had their children drink a cyanide-laced, Kool-Aid-type beverage and then drank it themselves. Apparently these cult devotees had been carefully coached to drink the 'Kool-Aid' in several pre-suicide rehearsals. Jones had promised these adepts, who had left the USA to follow him to Guyana, that they would enjoy the reward of a utopian life in Eden-like surroundings in exchange for obedient, loyal service.

Jones had, over time, prepared his followers saying if the outside world began to close in and interfere with their lives the only course left to them would be to all die - together. He assured them that upon death they would find themselves on another planet where they would live the promised utopian life.

They were primed to never question his authority, to blindly trust and immediately obey. The cult members had offered up their critical thinking skills and accepted whatever decisions Jones made for them. They were under the control of a savvy, unscrupulous confidence man disguised as a divinely-inspired saviour.

While horrified by this unfathomable tragedy, there was also an element of curiosity and intrigue for me, because I could see several parallels between the cult of Jim Jones' "Peoples Temple" and the sect of Jehovah's Witnesses, of which I was a member from birth. Of course the beliefs were not the same. Jehovah's Witnesses' leaders were not anywhere as extreme or as egomaniacal as Jones. The similarity seemed to be the use of certain manipulative control measures on the membership, and the members' blind acceptance of whatever pronouncements came from the top. There was also the willingness of followers to sacrifice their personal lives and devote themselves to the warped vision of a man - while in the case of the Jehovah's Witnesses, it was devotion and obedience to a group of men who called themselves the divinely-inspired, Governing Body of Jehovah's Witnesses.

December, 1978 - Montreal, Canada: My husband and I were raising our first child after having been special pioneers (full-time representatives) for the Watchtower Bible & Tract Society for over five years. Our daughter was almost six and the time had arrived where we were expected to seriously indoctrinate her and even coach her to speak to householders in the door-to-door ministry. I had already been a disinclined, unhappy member of the sect for years and was balking at the thought of having to train my daughter to do the very things I resented.

It was difficult for my husband (an elder and presiding overseer) to continue all his volunteer work for the Witness organization as he saw me pulling away. At some point, during that difficult period of my exit, he was counseled by fellow elders in the congregation to "*bring his rebellious wife into submission*". Terry, however, had never expected me to submit to his will as if I were inferior to him. There were only a few occasions where he encouraged me to try to do better with regard to all the Watchtower's expectations. One of those occasions was right after the Jonestown massacre.

As said, by about the age of about six the JW organization expected children (especially children of elders) to begin giving little comments at the meetings and to begin saying a few words when they accompanied their parents in the door-to-door work. I had been participating less and less in field service because I disliked it, but even more because I could not bear the hypocrisy of knocking on someone's door to preach about things I no longer believed myself. Now Terry was beginning to not only encourage me to go in field service but to take our little girl and begin to train her to speak at the doors as well.

There was an assembly scheduled for our circuit in the month of December, 1978. Before such assemblies, the circuit overseer (and back then the district overseer, as well) would spend a week with the host congregation - checking on their spiritual health - going in service with the congregants - giving extra little pep talks at the Kingdom Hall. Terry nudged me saying it would be a good thing if our daughter and I could go in the service, at least once, with the district and circuit overseer during this week of *"special activity"*. It would reflect badly on him, and he would be challenged about it if I, an elder's wife, did not make an appearance for field service during the week.

I was conflicted - and angry. Not angry at Terry so much as at the persistent, unreasonable expectations of the Watchtower organization. It felt as if I were being asked to take my daughter with me to rob a bank and there was no option but to comply. I went against my own inner knowing, against my own sense of what was right and prepared myself and our five year old for a morning of field service with the district overseer.

This field service outing became an inner struggle with what felt like an act of self-betrayal. My psyche was making the event into a threshold moment. What does it do to a person, I wondered, to keep acting against their own inner knowing? Why could I not stand up for myself and what I wanted to do and not do? What was I doing to myself and my family by allowing this crazy-making, inner conflict to continue? Bizarrely, regardless of what I was thinking, feeling, wanting, there was at the same time a strong, inner imperative to push myself to do what was expected of me. What does that oft-quoted scripture at Proverbs 22:6 say? *"Train up a child in the way he should go, and when he is old, he will not depart from it."* Yes, I had been well trained and was now having trouble departing from the training – even though I wanted to!

It was a dreary day and my daughter and I were assigned to work on the opposite side of the street from the district overseer and his witnessing companion. Feeling dreadful, hating myself for this act of self-betrayal and hypocrisy, being on the verge of crying, I decided to not put my daughter or any householder through seeing me burst into tears at the door. The only thing I could think of was to go to every door, pretend to ring the doorbell, but not actually ring it. After going to every door on our side of the street and only pretending to ring the doorbells, the district overseer, Brother L.C., approached us to ask how it went. I mumbled something about how hard it was to find anyone at home because so many people had full-time jobs.

Finally this dreadful morning came to an end and we went home. I fed my daughter lunch and got her off on the school bus for her afternoon of Kindergarten. After closing the door, I leaned against it, slid down collapsing in a heap on the floor, sobbing in desperation and hopelessness. That moment was one of the lowest points of my life. I did not feel able to fight or flee. I froze.

"These pains you feel are messengers. Listen to them." ~Rumi

Following close on the heels of both the Jonestown mass suicide and that day of self-betrayal and hopelessness was our circuit assembly. It was becoming more evident to me that the Watchtower did exert a subtle form of thought-control over its rank and file. The difficulty I had in listening to and acting upon my own thoughts about participating in field service was evidence of that. The shocking events of the "Peoples Temple" cult solidified the growing imperative I felt to protect my child from any further exposure to, and indoctrination by, a fundamentalist group. But still, I caved to external demands and to my own internalized expectations (carefully crafted by the Watchtower organization) and attended this circuit assembly.

There were about 1000 people in attendance at the Sunday public talk, given by this same district overseer. (This was approximately the same number of people, gathered at an assembly of Jehovah's Witnesses, as were conned and killed by Jim Jones in Guyana one month earlier.) I sat alone in the audience with my daughter, as my husband was always busy organizing the assembly behind the scenes. A couple of short talks were delivered by other brothers after the main discourse, and then a brother re-introduced District Overseer L.C. to deliver the closing talk of this French circuit assembly:

Brother: *Let's give a warm welcome back to the platform for our dear District Overseer, Brother L.C.* (The brother who made this introduction then left the stage to attend to other assembly business.)

Audience: *Applause ...*

As the audience applause began to die down, the platform remained empty. Brother L.C. had not made his way to the podium. The brothers and sisters in the audience began to feel uncomfortable, shifted in their seats and looked around. Whispers could be heard around the large auditorium. Still ... no one appeared on the platform ...

Now if you have attended any conventions or large meetings, be they secular or religious, you know that a stage or platform is never left empty for long because it makes an audience decidedly anxious. The longer there is no one at the podium leading the group, the more uncomfortable they become. This is exactly what was happening here. I began to wonder if Brother L.C. had had to make an unexpected trip to the men's room. As the stage continued to be vacant, I even wondered if he had become ill. Had he fainted? Had he had a heart attack? I know I was not alone with those thoughts. People continued to stir in their seats. The silence, with no one speaking from the platform, dominated the large room.

To the relief of us all, Brother L.C., our middle-aged, balding district overseer, finally ran up the stairs of the stage and took his place, breathlessly, behind the podium, and said (translated from French) something very close to the following:

District Overseer, L.C.: *"Forgive me dear brothers and sisters,* (huffing and puffing) *I would never leave you hanging, waiting like this, if it were not* **vitally important**. *I just got off the phone with Bethel* (pant, pant, pant) *and, would you believe,* **I've been told that the Governing Body has determined the exact date on which the Great Tribulation will begin!!!"**

Audience: *...* began to *tentatively applaud* ... slowly the *applause got louder* ... parts of the audience began to get to their feet while applauding ... the applause became more vigorous ...

I did not applaud. I was stunned by L.C.'s statement and even more stunned by the audience reaction to it. I turned around and looked with disbelief at the brothers and sisters, many my friends, who were applauding enthusiastically in spite of knowing the scripture that had been drummed into our heads: *"But concerning that day and hour no one knows, not even the angels of heaven, nor the Son, but the Father only."* Matthew 24:36. Almost every member of the audience knew that scripture and yet when this district overseer told them that Bethel had now determined the exact date the Great Tribulation would begin, they ignored what they knew and greeted with excited applause, what they thought was the about-to-be-announced date of the beginning of the end. What was going on?!

District Overseer, L.C. interrupted the enthusiastic applause and began to speak again, saying something to the effect of: "*Brothers! Sisters! Please ... Please stop applauding! (long pause for effect) My brothers and sisters,* **what are you thinking?! What are you doing?!** *You know full well that Jesus said "no one knows the day or the hour!" Why would you override what Jesus tells us in Matthew 24:36 and welcome my surprising declaration to you?* **Really – what are you thinking?"**

Yes. This district overseer had cunningly planned and executed this stunt as a sort of test, and the brothers and sisters at this assembly had failed - miserably. He then chastised them from the platform for 'their failure'. He shamed them for the reaction he had so calculatingly contrived.

The majority of people in attendance at that assembly had done what is described so clearly by Christopher Hitchens: "*To 'choose' dogma and faith over doubt and experience is to throw out the ripening vintage and to reach greedily for the Kool-Aid.*" Metaphorically the audience at that December assembly drank the Kool-Aid.

L.C. finished this final talk of the assembly, which he had turned into a scolding, reproachful lecture. Before long we were singing the closing song and hearing the closing prayer. The brothers and sisters packed up their bags, gathered their children, put on their coats and said their goodbyes in a somber, deflated mood. It was surreal. I can only imagine that they must have been experiencing a tremendous amount of confusion, cognitive dissonance, and shame. No doubt they were trying to internally process what had happened. There seemed to be a tacit agreement that there would be no discussions about the shocking event that had just transpired. It was the quietest after-assembly departure scene I had ever seen. Was everyone silently wrestling with the evidence they might be victims of mind-control, or at the very least, serious manipulation? I figured my husband must have had a close-up view of the district overseer's contrived antics from the assembly hall office, and couldn't wait to hear his opinion about the whole fiasco on our drive home:

Me: *So what was everyone saying back in the office about what L.C. did?*
Terry: *L.C.? What did he do?*
Me: *What did he do?! You didn't hear him?*
Terry: *No.*
Me: *No one told you?!*
Terry: *No.*
Me: I proceeded to tell him what happened, just as described above.
Terry: *Come on, he really said that? Are you sure you didn't misunderstand?*
Me: *I did NOT misunderstand, and neither did anyone else in the auditorium!*
Terry: *Well, if that is what he did he will be severely reprimanded by Bethel. He should not have put the brothers to the test like that, and he certainly should not have shamed them about their reaction.*
Me: *What about what the audience did? What about how, in a split second, they were willing to forget everything they had ever learned from the Bible, from the Society and accept L.C.'s statement that the Governing Body now knows the day and the hour?! Doesn't the audience reaction concern you?*
Terry: *Yea .... what on earth were they thinking?*
Me: *That's just it ... we've been trained not to think ... we've been trained to accept whatever is fed to us from The Watchtower or from the podium or by an elder! Are we being controlled even more than we realize?*
Terry: *silence .... Well don't worry, L.C. will really be called on the carpet for this.*
Me: *I don't care what happens to L.C.! I care about how we have been groomed to be so malleable and compliant - how we are under the control of the brothers at the top - how we will believe and likely do whatever they tell us! It's just like The People's Temple! The vast majority of the brothers and sisters in that room today drank L.C.'s Kool-Aid!*
Terry: *Come on now ... that's a bit extreme.*

I didn't let Terry's rather defensive responses bother me at that moment, because even though I was traumatized by the L.C. 'Kool-Aid' scenario, all my gut feelings had actually been affirmed by it. I'd just seen concrete evidence of my secret suspicions that we rank and file Jehovah's Witnesses had been carefully groomed to swallow whatever poisonous offerings the Governing Body or its representatives put before us. The whole pitiful scene was proof that we had been trained to bury our critical thinking faculties. Like Jim Jones' followers we were really at the mercy of whatever the leaders of this organization wanted us to believe or do.

The incident was a pivotal confirmation of all of my concerns. That circuit assembly spectacle propelled me even deeper into my knowing, on every level that mattered, that I could no longer be a member of this high-control sect. (I could not, however, bring myself to think of it or name it expressly as a cult at that time.)

There was no internet then. There was no one (that I knew of) publishing information about the Watchtower - revealing the contradictions, the duplicity, the lies, the hypocrisy, the exploitation, or that exposed them for the dangerous, high-control group that they were. There were no iPhones with which someone in the crowd could have videoed the whole eye-opening scene. The scene would never be digitally uploaded to a public forum for all to see. Well, my eyes, ears, mind and heart recorded it. The entire episode is seared in my memory as incontrovertible proof of JW mind-control. I am 'uploading' it to you now, exactly as I have had it locked in memory for more than thirty years. What a 'stroke of luck' to have seen the effects of JW mind-manipulation in action with my own eyes! Thank you, Brother L.C. Your perverse hoax was ultimately a gift for anyone still in possession of some critical thinking faculties.

I'll never know if that afternoon became a tipping point for anyone else. It's my guess that the majority in attendance could not allow themselves to realize the true import of what happened. They probably automatically suppressed any information or situation that could shake up their faith-based world view. It's hard to let in information that creates cognitive dissonance and demonstrates that you may have bought into a lie, that you may have wasted your time, your life, and that you may have been unwittingly complicit in misleading your own children.

District overseer L.C.'s ruse was a critical moment in my understanding that I had to find a way to leave the Jehovah's Witness sect. It would still take a bit more time before my physical body was completely out. It was, however, the moment when my mind and heart checked out.

Along with concerns about being trapped in a high-control sect, being expected to now indoctrinate my daughter and the betrayal of my own inner knowing, another worry was that my husband and I were not on the same page in the way we perceived the Watchtower organization, as evidenced in our conversation after that assembly. Terry played a prominent role in the JW sect in our area and it would be quite scandalous should he ever decide to leave. This contributed to the difficulty figuring out when and exactly how I could leave. It seemed highly probable that I would have to leave alone. What that would mean for our marriage and our life was not easy to contemplate. Leaving that religion would put a lot at stake – like my daughter's intact family.

But let's go back to the beginning so you can understand the background, upbringing, experiences and influences that brought me to that dramatic December, 1978 decision to finally end my involvement with the Jehovah's Witness organization and, thereby, jeopardize my marriage, endanger my daughter's stable family, and risk precious bonds with my JW family of origin.

We would rather be ruined than changed.
We would rather die in our dread
Than climb the cross of the present
And let our illusions die.
~W.H. Auden

CHAPTER 3

Beginnings Explain a Lot

My family's association with Jehovah's Witnesses stretches back four generations on my mother's side and three generations on my father's side. My father was a reluctant Witness, who soon after marriage to my mother, became an inactive one. My mother on the other hand was an ever-enthusiastic devotee. Let me begin with my father, Irvine MacEwan.

Irvine was the first child of young parents who emigrated from Scotland to Canada. From what I've been told, Irvine's father, John MacEwan began his involvement with the Bible Student movement shortly after the tragic death of his young wife. She died of pneumonia soon after giving birth to their third son, Clifford.

The story goes that once John MacEwan discovered the writings of Charles Taze Russell in the nineteen-twenties, he was eager to spread *"the good news"* in Canada. In order to devote his time to proselytizing in Northern Ontario he decided to travel from town to town in a sort of camper-trailer that they called *"house-cars"*. Many of these house-cars were equipped with sound systems to grab the attention of people as they rolled into town. These travelling preachers (colporteurs) slept in the back of the house-cars as they travelled spreading *"the good news of the kingdom"* message.

But, didn't I just say that John MacEwan had three motherless sons? To be free to travel from place to place preaching *"the good news of the kingdom"*, John placed his three young sons in an orphanage - more than once. What kind of a father does a thing like that? How does a father, whose sons have already lost their mother, justify leaving them in an institution so he can engage in the preaching work and think that is something a loving God would want? I cannot fathom such a decision. But that is the one my grandfather made. It was an ill-advised, selfish choice having repercussions that rippled down to affect future generations.

My father, Irvine, being the eldest of these three little boys, did his best to look out for his two younger brothers when placed in the orphanage. When his little brothers were punished (sometimes beaten) for disobedience, crying, or wetting their beds in the orphanage, my father would bundle them up and run away. What a desperate, courageous act for a little boy. I do not know where he ran to, or how he knew where to find my proselytizing grandfather. I do know that one good-hearted Jehovah's Witness brother named Walt Furlong, seeing the plight of these three boys and the irresponsibility of their father, took the youngest boy Clifford, under his wing and was instrumental in helping to raise him. The other two boys, Irvine and Nelson, were apparently left to their own devices. As adults neither were interested in following in their father's proselytizing footsteps. Clifford MacEwan, who had enjoyed the guidance of JW Walt Furlong continued as a Jehovah's Witness throughout his life.

My mother had little respect for her father-in-law, John MacEwan, based on the many things she learned about him, including this neglect of his three boys in order to engage in the witnessing work. (By the way, neglect of children is now legally considered a form of abuse.) Mom told me the following story about my grandfather, John MacEwan, as related to her by my father:

When Irvine was a little older (a pre-teen) and perhaps my grandfather was by this time disenchanted with the "colporteur" adventure, my grandfather ordered Irvine to go out alone in the preaching work - regardless of the harsh winter weather in Northern Ontario. My father was assigned several large blocks of a town where he had to go and leave tracts at each and every door. Even though it was the dead of winter he was not allowed to return home until he had completed the task. Once he returned home from one of these miserable, bitter, lonely assignments with frostbite. Irvine, thereby, developed a real distaste for the witnessing work, an abiding resentment of the Watchtower Society and probably of his father as well.

When they were older, the three boys called my grandfather, John MacEwan, "*the old buck*". My mother said that my paternal grandfather had a clever mind and one way he used this intelligence was to outsmart the Bible Student Association. He had several questionable liaisons with different women during his 'colporteur' travels which, of course, went against the moral code of the "*Bible Students*". His unique and persuasive approach for sharing the good news of the kingdom really helped some women see the light! John MacEwan managed to never be reproved by the organization for these cunning 'conversions'. He was apparently too crafty to be caught or reproved by them - or if caught, he managed to talk his way out of any reproof. His penchant for the ladies was surely where the moniker "*the old buck*" came from. Mom always said my paternal grandfather "*should have been a lawyer*".

Based on this negligent upbringing by a careless, selfish, often absent, yet bizarrely pious single father, my father developed the habit of running away when life got tough. Who could blame him as a child? Unfortunately, it became a habit he could not break as an adult.

Young Irvine MacEwan visiting the Manitoulin Island where he met my mother, Clara Hodgson.

When my father met my mother, Clara Hodgson, with her passionate love of life, her ability to find pleasure in the simplest of things, her great sense of humour and her immediate infatuation with him, it was surely a balm that soothed many unmet needs from his forsaken, lonely childhood. I assume they must have met due to their mutual connections to the Bible Student movement soon to be known as Jehovah's Witnesses.

Clara's mother Rose, and her five children, were introduced to the teachings of Charles Taze Russell by tracts sent to her by her father while he was travelling in the United States. My great-grandfather was transfixed by Pastor Russell after hearing some of his rousing sermons during that trip to the States. Rose and her husband John lived on the Manitoulin Island in Lake Huron, in Ontario, Canada. My maternal grandfather, also named John (John Hodgson) was never really interested in the Bible Student movement. I'm not sure if there were other people on the Manitoulin Island interested in this new, 'millennial' Christian sect in the 1920s or 1930s. There was no congregation there at that time. The Bible Students probably gathered together to study, pray and plan their next proselytizing circuits, in private homes. Most of my mother's many relatives living on the Manitoulin Island eventually became Jehovah's Witnesses.

While still in her late teens my mother met a woman who came to the Manitoulin Island in one of those JW house-cars to distribute the tracts published by this new religious movement. This woman, Grace Lonsbury, (her real name) had been touring the island and the Northern Ontario regions and invited my young, eager mother to join her. Grace Lonsbury was known for her devotion to the preaching work and my mother felt honored to be able to accompany her and learn from her. Mom was an enthusiastic colporteur right from the start.

Soon after my father and mother met, they moved separately to the city of Toronto, Ontario. Mom wanted to be where the Jehovah's Witnesses had Kingdom Halls and regular meetings. She also wanted to participate with other Witnesses in the preaching work. My paternal grandfather and my father's brother, Clifford were by then living in Toronto so it made sense for my father to move there too. Since my father loved cars, and was already a proficient mechanic, he knew there would be more work opportunities for him in Toronto.

Before leaving the Manitoulin Island, Mom learned how to cook in a professional kitchen while working at the Red Cross Hospital in the small town of Mindemoya (a lot of the towns on the Manitoulin Island had native American names). It was at that little hospital that she earned the money to be able to move to Toronto and fulfill her dream of belonging to a real congregation and participating in all its activities. She then used those culinary skills to work as a private cook in well-to-do homes in Toronto.

Both of my parents, having grown-up during the Great Depression, followed closely by their coming of age at the outbreak of World War II, like most of their generation, must not have felt very optimistic about their future. The Jehovah's Witness beliefs of their parents offered some hope that the suffering, deprivations and seeming dead-ends of that tumultuous time would dissolve with the soon to be established earthly paradise. Unstable, frightening world conditions had set them up to easily adopt a belief system that seduced them with the promise they could survive God's imminent intervention in world affairs and actually live forever on a paradise earth. It gave them hope and purpose. It gave my mother community. There was no thought given to the price they might have to pay to 'purchase' such guarantees of a perfect future ... and clearly no thought as to how it would affect their relationship or any future children. The supposed Bible-based promises of this new 'movement' seemed heaven-sent and they (especially my mother) optimistically climbed aboard the Jehovah's Witness express.

My father, called "Mac" by everyone but my mother, was a skilled mechanic and could always find work wherever he travelled.

CHAPTER 4

Mom & Dad - For Better

Once in Toronto my mother was invited by an older sister (originally from Finland) Lena Peko, who owned and operated a Finnish-style steam bath and massage business, to live and work with her. This was an offer my mother could not refuse. Why Jehovah was providing for her already!

While living with this rather gruff, yet kind and generous woman (and being put on strict regimens of grape cleanses and cabbage soup diets) my mother learned how to give deep tissue body massages. Some of JW Lena Peko's clients at her Finnish steam bath were brothers from the leadership of the Canadian Headquarters of the Watchtower Bible & Tract Society also known as Toronto Bethel. The Toronto Bethel was in the central part of the city at that time, as was Lena's steam bath. I have a strong recollection of Mom telling me that Lena assigned her to give massages to well-known Toronto Bethelites, and I've often wondered if Percy Chapman the Branch Servant, and Leo Greenlees, another Toronto bethelite, were among them. I wonder because long-standing stories among Jehovah's Witnesses themselves, allege that Branch Servant Percy Chapman and Leo Greenlees had a long-term sexual relationship at Toronto Bethel. As well, a Kingdom Hall on Irwin Avenue in Toronto (in the middle of Toronto's gay district at that time) was situated above a gay nightclub. It is rumoured that Percy Chapman, followed by young male bethelite companions, would regularly descend downstairs, directly after the meeting, to frequent the club. Years later when the president of the Watchtower, Nathan H. Knorr, learned of the relationship between Chapman and Greenlees, Percy Chapman was demoted from his position as

Bethel Servant to that of a janitor in the Toronto headquarters, and it is said he was ordered by Knorr to marry. Leo Greenlees, however, was transferred from Toronto Bethel to Brooklyn Bethel. Greenlees became a member of the Governing Body while serving in Brooklyn, but was asked to leave both the Governing Body and Bethel when an accusation arose that he had molested a young JW boy. (The boy and his parents made the accusation and have spoken publicly about it.) Referencing immoral practices within the Watchtower organization, that had become public knowledge and therefore, finally had to be addressed, the Watchtower Magazine of January 1, 1986 said, "*Shocking as it is, even some who have been prominent in Jehovah's organization have succumbed to immoral practices, including homosexuality, wife swapping, and child molesting.*"

From left to right: Leo Greenlees, Bethelite; Glen How, Lawyer; Nathan Knorr, Pres. WBTS; Percy Chapman, Canadian Branch Servant; Montreal 1947, a few years after the time my mother worked in the steam bath frequented by some members of the Canadian Headquarters, and several years before Knorr learned of the alleged liaison between Leo and Percy. (Image: prawdziweobliczewts.info)

If my mother heard of the alleged, unbiblical proclivities of some of her massage clients from Toronto Bethel, she kept the information to herself. Had she heard any insinuations, I think she would have dismissed them as highly unlikely. The above rumours (intermingled with known facts) are difficult to definitively substantiate but they are prolific, consistent, and partially confirmed. It is my opinion, therefore, that they need to be referenced here to demonstrate the zeitgeist existing in the JW leadership in Toronto at that time. (Both Chapman and Greenlees are dead and neither left behind any offspring who could be hurt by reading about the claims here.) The rumours are pertinent to my mother's life as a Jehovah's Witness and a massage therapist in Toronto at that time. Those possible secret activities at the Canadian Bethel from the late thirties to early sixties belie the morally upright reputation of the organization in which she had so eagerly and confidently placed her trust. Mom looked up to, listened to Biblical exhortations from, and associated with both Percy Chapman and Leo Greenlees. I, too, knew Leo Greenlees as a child in the city of Toronto in the early sixties. Leo was a much admired brother in our circuit and the city.

Mom intermingled with all levels of Jehovah's Witnesses: - while working for Sister Peko - at the meetings she faithfully attended - and in the distribution of Watchtower pamphlets and books around the city of Toronto. She happily immersed herself in all the activities of the sect. When she was not working at the steam bath to pay for her room and board, she was out pounding the pavement with placards (aka sandwich boards) strapped on her body that announced the imminent end of the world, or standing on street corners offering Bible-based pamphlets and magazines announcing the coming establishment of Jehovah God's kingdom. My mother had found her mission in life with the Jehovah's Witnesses and the love of her life in my father. Unfortunately for my mother, my father was never able to develop the same enthusiasm for this religion and all its proselytizing activities.

A letter, dated March 28th, 1938 from 61 Foxbar Road, Toronto indicating that my mother was leaving a place of employment to "*take up religious work in which she is, very much interested*" affirms her devotion to the Witnesses. She would have been nineteen years old, unmarried, and passionate about her service to Jehovah at the time this reference letter was written. Since Mom died in 2009, and had already been going door-to-door as a Witness before she arrived in Toronto, we can extrapolate that she gave almost seventy-five years of her life in service to the Watchtower Bible & Tract Society. Near the end of her life, she must have been proud of that record and fully expecting to survive the Battle of Armageddon and live in the long-promised paradise under Christ's kingdom rule. The phrase "*a fool's dream*" just popped unbidden in my head and yet no one, including me, would have considered my mother "a fool".

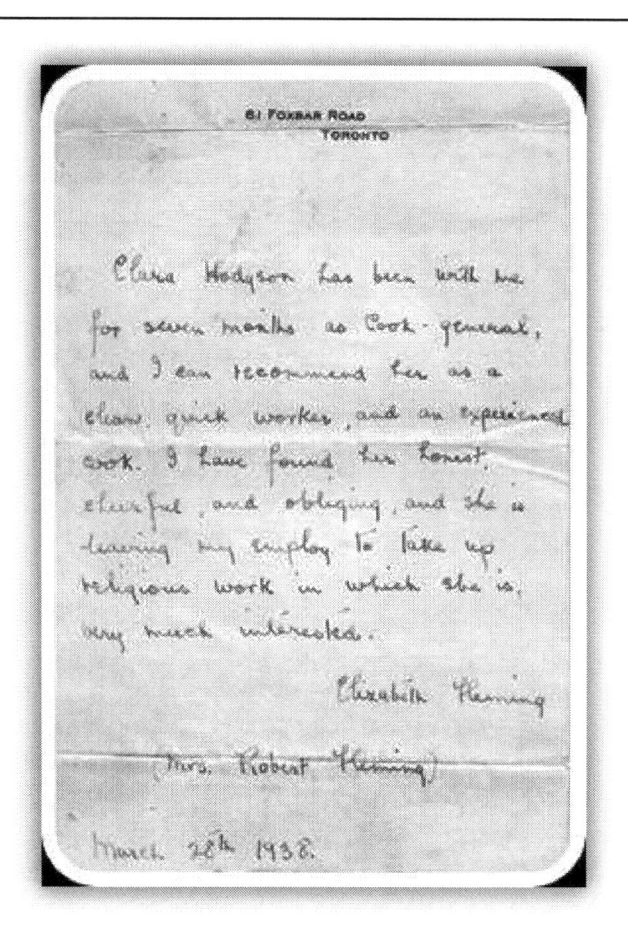

> 61 FOXBAR ROAD
> TORONTO
>
> Clara Hodgson has been with me for seven months as Cook-general, and I can recommend her as a clean, quick worker, and an experienced cook. I have found her honest, cheerful, and obliging, and she is leaving my employ to take up religious work in which she is very much interested.
>
> Elizabeth Fleming
> (Mrs. Robert Fleming)
>
> March 28th 1938.

Mom told me when she first arrived in Toronto from the Manitoulin Island, she went to an assembly of Jehovah's Witnesses at a well-known center for the performing arts in Toronto called Massey Hall. (Massey Hall is still a popular venue for live entertainment in Toronto to this day and seats about 3,000 people. My father's mother, a concert pianist, had performed there before my father or mother were born.) So strong was her delight at hearing the Biblical message from the Bible Student or Witness speaker on the stage, she clapped after almost everything he said - often being the only person in the large audience applauding. Mom's descriptions of meetings, conventions and field service never made mention of my father being with her.

Single Clara after her move to Toronto.

Even though my father was a reluctant, peripheral Jehovah's Witness and my mother an ever-eager, involved one, their personal attraction and love grew. In their case, opposites truly did attract. They married during the Second World War on Christmas Day, 1941. Around that time, the then president of the Watchtower organization, Judge Rutherford, had blatantly suggested that because the end-of-times was *so* near, good Christians would surely want to put off marriage and child-rearing and concentrate their energies in the preaching work. (Yes, Armageddon was right around the corner back in the nineteen-forties, too!) That exhortation from Rutherford was just fine with my father. Although he and my mother ignored the part to not marry, my father was happy to delay having children because he wanted to see the world and experience a free, unfettered life with his partner.

Clara & Irvine's wedding photograph.

Soon after their marriage, my father appealed to my mother's love of him and love of good times, persuading her to leave all the Jehovah's Witness activities in Toronto to set out on a life of travel and adventure. They took off, travelling wherever their inclinations took them.

Mom always had a little streak of rebelliousness - so they set out on what ended up being over six years of adventures that took them away from all JW contact and influence. At some point during the war my father was briefly interned at a prison camp at Chalk River (Petawawa) Ontario for conscientious objectors who refused to be conscripted into the war. I'm not sure if it was truly a matter of Christian conscience for him, or if he simply preferred the experience of internment to the experience of war. Who wouldn't? I do recall that my mother took advantage of that brief time period, separated from her husband, to pioneer.

She was visiting alone at the home of her father-in-law, John MacEwan, when she came down with the chills and fever of what was eventually diagnosed as pneumonia. My grandfather must have offered her his bed and then proceeded to go about his day. After hours alone in his bed, raging with fever, my mother weakly called for someone to bring her something to drink. No one responded. Hours passed with no one checking in on her. Finally it seemed that a drink of water was becoming a matter of life or death. In her desperation, Mom did the only thing she could do. She grabbed a glass of murky water on her father-in-law's bedside table and drank every drop. It was the water in which his false teeth were soaking at the time! In spite of ingesting something so vile, she recovered. That episode of gross neglect was a chance for her to experience firsthand her father-in-law's self-centeredness and his ability to disregard those around him who were in need, as he had years before with his three boys.

(Another earlier example of my grandfather MacEwan's neglect of those under his care: At one point, he was "*living in sin*" with a worldly woman - a woman he met, perhaps, during his colporteur adventures - I'm not sure. She had a young daughter (Jean) in the same age range as my grandfather's three boys. Though this woman and my grandfather were not married, his boys considered Jean to be their 'step-sister'. One December evening, the four young children were left at home alone and decided to entertain themselves by playing a game inspired by the old children's rhyme, "*Jack be nimble. Jack be quick. Jack jump over the candlestick.*" As they took their turns jumping over *a* lit candle, the only girl, Jean, jumped over - but her long nightgown did not clear the flame. Before any of the boys (including my father) knew what had happened, Jean was engulfed in flames. The three boys did their best to extinguish the flames on her legs, arms and body – but she ended up with severe third degree burns. Only her face was spared. Where were the parents of this group of young children? Out visiting? At a JW meeting? Out conducting a Bible study? I don't have that information. Jean bore the physical and emotional pain and scars of that parental neglect for the rest of her life. The three young boys who witnessed her go up in flames and worked to put them out, also bore the trauma of the event for the rest of their lives. And the parents ... must surely have had to live with the guilt of the terrible consequences of neglecting their young, active children. I met my father's step-sister, Jean, only twice. She always wore long-sleeve and high-neck sweaters or blouses to hide her shriveled, leathery, rigid skin. It's no surprise that my grandfather was never able to convince her, or her mother, to become Jehovah's Witnesses.)

Back to my parent's story: Dad, though married and now reunited with my mother after his wartime internment and her bout with pneumonia, had no intention of being tied down to a nine to five job. He needed to be free. Mom always said he was born in the wrong time period and should have been a nineteenth-century explorer. They started out with plans to travel across Canada. They had no savings, no jobs and no accommodations waiting for them anywhere. When they needed money they would find itinerant work. They picked grapes in Ontario wine country. They picked apples in the Okanogan Valley in British Columbia. When my father heard he could make good money at a logging camp in northern British Columbia, they headed north. While he was logging, Mom became the cook for the entire logging camp. She was the only female there. Surprisingly, I don't recall her telling any stories of trying to proselytize during any of their travelling adventures. They were just enjoying life, the beautiful planet and each other. These were the best times of their lives.

One of the burly loggers at the camp dared Mom to accompany him in a small boat or canoe while he 'shot the rapids' that ushered the giant logs down to a collection area at the base of the mountain. She didn't think twice. Even though she could not swim and was afraid of water, she was up for the challenge and jumped in. She bragged about that experience for the rest of her life.

At one point after they had moved on from the logging camp, as the weather turned cold, my parents decided that hitch-hiking was no longer the way to go. Why not hop aboard freight trains as … 'non-paying customers'? It would be much warmer to be huddled together in a freight car than to stand on the side of the road in rain, sleet, or snow with their thumbs in the wind. My father was concerned they might encounter other 'non-paying customers' (invariably male) in the boxcars and encouraged my mother to disguise herself as a man. So Mom happily cross-dressed, tucking her hair up under a man's cap while wearing men's overalls, shirts and boots. A bizarre way to live, but it's what they wanted to do and, as the photograph shows, they had fun doing it.

Clara & Irvine, in transit on the rails, with no family, property, jobs or religious commitments to encumber their quest for adventure. Here my Mother is dressed in my Father's mechanic overalls. I think the lopsided cap on his head (which she probably plopped there just before the photograph was taken) was actually the one she wore and under which she tucked up her long hair. My Mom, a happy cross-dresser!

All this travelling back and forth across the country did not allow my mother to connect with any Jehovah's Witnesses, attend any meetings, or participate in the preaching work. But the allure of the Witnesses could not, at that time, match the pull of travelling with the man she loved. Oh yes, I forgot to mention that one scorching, hot summer during their six years of blissful freedom, they lived mainly in the buff on a deserted island in Georgian Bay (a bay in Lake Huron). My parents were hippies before the term existed! They didn't drink. They didn't use drugs. They were just high on each other, high on nature, high on freedom and high on life. Mom loved to recount their many free-spirited, romantic adventures to her two daughters in later years. How she then turned around and traded such freedom and happiness for servitude to the Watchtower Society boggles my mind. It must have boggled the mind of my father too.

CHAPTER 5

Baby Breaks the Spell

After six years of a carefree life with no rules but the ones they embraced, my mother discovered she was pregnant and had the natural urge to settle down and make a home for her baby. Of course, the worst words my father could hear were "*it's time to settle down*". It was the death-knell for freedom and adventure with the woman he loved. Baby Bonnie came along and broke the spell.

Mom knew she must not demand too much of my father. To settle down and earn a living was going to be a difficult lifestyle change for him. She knew he was not interested in, or even prepared to handle much responsibility. Knowing that, she asked for so very little and, sad to say, that is exactly what she got. Their first somewhat permanent home was a cramped, one-room, uninsulated, residential garage in a town called Lakeview on the outskirts of Toronto.

Their baby was born at Women's College Street Hospital in Toronto and brought back to the one-room, detached garage in Lakeview. Mom says she rarely put me in my drawer (the only crib they could afford), because she felt she needed to hold me all the time to keep me from crying. My father had difficulty tolerating the noise of a crying baby and there was nowhere he could go to escape it. She lived fearing that, in spite of their connection, he might choose his love of adventure over his love for her their new baby.

It was at this point that my mother resumed her association with the Jehovah's Witnesses. She was, perhaps, seeking some stability and predictability in her life. She had a good mind and being a Witness gave her literature to study and concepts to mull over. But above all she wanted to prepare the ground for raising her daughter "in the truth". My father was friendly with the Witnesses but attended few meetings and did not go in what they called 'the work' seeking to make new converts.

Soon we outgrew the one-room garage and moved to Scollard Street in the downtown Toronto neighborhood known now as Yorkville. It was Yorkville before Yorkville became hip with the nightclub crowd, and later gentrified and upscale. My father started up his own car repair business and my mother let out rooms in their house to earn extra money.

One of my first memories of my mother is in the kitchen of that house on Scollard Street. I was probably about eighteen months old and must have been looking up at her from a high chair. I knew something was wrong. She did not look like my Mommy. Her face was swollen, her mouth caved in, she seemed unable to talk to me and was clearly in pain. I was frightened. Bad things aren't supposed to happen to your mother.

Years later Mom explained that scary memory to me: She began to have one problem after another with her teeth, necessitating frequent, expensive visits to the dentist. My father was annoyed by the mounting dentist bills and expressed his frustration to my mother. So in a foolish, impulsive attempt to prevent more dentist bills and appease my father, Mom asked the dentist to remove all of her teeth. All her teeth were removed in one sitting where she had been rendered unconscious using gas. She arrived home from that horrific session having to make a large evening meal for all the boarders and to care for her toddler. What a drastic, irreversible decision by my mother - to accommodate my father. It was a decision she always regretted and one that, at the time, terrified her little girl.

While I have no memory of going to meetings or in service with my mother at that time, I'm sure accompanying her in these activities was part of my weekly routine. I've always wondered how much actual indoctrination takes place in the mind of a small toddler present at all those meetings. An incident a couple of years later reveals that my little mind was being well-indoctrinated in JW concepts. But we'll get to that later.

Around this time my father felt he was due for his next adventure, or perhaps he felt the need to run away from the pressures of his now domesticated life, or perhaps from pressure from Mom to join her in JW activities – who knows. Since taking a baby along was not an option, he decided to go on this adventure alone. Mom found a note on her pillow saying he had gone to Mexico and did not know when he would be back. He just took off, leaving her with a child, a boarding house, and all the commitments of his new car repair shop. Mom had to find ways to meet all the household expenses and was especially concerned about paying creditors of my father's business so that it would still be viable for him when he returned. I recall her saying that she paid some of them with fifty cents or a dollar to demonstrate good faith and because she could not afford more.

This disappearing/reappearing behavior was becoming a pattern with my father and, as said, was probably a factor in solidifying my mother's tight allegiance to the Jehovah's Witness religion. In the unpredictable life with my Father, JW activities were always something she could count on. The meetings, the publications, the door-to-door ministry, and the brothers and sisters were always there for her – unlike my Dad.

Mom was a complex woman. Well, we are all complex of course, but allow me to tell you about some of my mother's particular complexities. While there was a part of her that was a free-spirit, as evidenced by her six plus years of married life before they became parents, another part of her was a bit self-conscious and she had a few well-hidden insecurities especially now that she was a young woman wearing new false teeth. She viewed herself as a country girl who did not quite measure up to her city-slicker sisters in the truth. Because of this, she was quite preoccupied with creating a good impression of herself and her family with all and sundry. She actually did quite well in this regard, always dressing in the latest styles and looking quite fashionable, or *"spiffy"* as she would say.

Add to her own need to create a good impression, there was the Watchtower's frequent exhortations that Witnesses must set a *"good example"*, leave a *"good impression"* and never bring reproach on the name of Jehovah. To do so, Watchtower said, could mean turning a good heart toward the faith. All of this meant that image and impressions became quite an important theme for my mother ... and as a consequence, for her children.

"Don't turn away. Keep your gaze on the bandaged place. That's where the light enters you." ~Rumi

Mom also made sure, once she had children, that we were always coiffed and dressed to create that good impression. She sewed lovely little dresses and coats for us. She curled my hair every day, always making sure that I was *"cute as a button"* (her words) for meetings and service. She enjoyed the compliments that came her way about her little girls. And yet, in spite of her insecurities, she had a wonderful self-deprecating sense of humor as evidenced by the following field service story that she loved to tell.

Mom with me cautiously sitting on a pony.

CHAPTER 6

Early Indoctrination & Impressions

It was a Saturday and Mom planned to spend the morning standing at a busy intersection in downtown Toronto offering passersby the Watchtower and Awake! magazines. She dressed me in a smocked, white cotton dress she had recently made. While walking to the corner where we would stand, she encouraged me to be her *"good little girl"*, and decided a bribe could not hurt. We went into a corner store and she said I could choose any candy I wanted and eat it while Mommy talked to all the nice people. I chose a package of grape-flavored stick gum.

Later as she tried to interest people in the magazines and talked to the few who took time to stop and chat, she could not help but notice that many of them would look at her *"adorable"* little daughter and then look up at her and smile. She swelled with pride knowing that her 'little darling' was creating that all important good impression for herself ... and Jehovah. At some point she bent down to speak with me and saw the real reason that people had been smiling at her. Her *"good little girl"* had stuffed the entire package of six sticks of grape gum into her little mouth. Ugly purple drool streamed down both sides of my chin, dripping off to puddle on and stain my white dress. When I smiled at her she saw that all my teeth where stained a disgusting tone of purple/grey, while bulges of purple gum protruded between the gaps in my teeth. Ah, those good intentions to create good impressions. I have no actual memories of this incident. I remember only my mother telling the story to friends and family and heartily laughing at the irony of it all.

Back then the Witnesses used to parade up and down streets (especially to advertise up-coming conventions) wearing cardboard signs (sandwich boards) announcing the title of the main talks and where and when they would be held. They called these cardboard signs "*placards*" and wore one on their front and one on their back – all held in place by strings. Mom must have imagined it would look cute if her little daughter wore a placard too. They must have had to adjust the size of the placards on my front and back to fit a child's body. Whatever adjustment was made it was not enough because we had only walked a few blocks handing out invitations to the public talk advertised on the placards, when blood began to drip down over the print on the front board. The cardboard had been creeping up my chest, finally nestling under my chin where it made a deep cut. Mom's efforts to advertise for the Watchtower with a cute little toddler always seemed to backfire on her!

Another incident a couple of years later demonstrates how even though my mother loved "*the truth*", she was never totally under its control. This story is actually a very good example of the constant inner dialectic of espoused values (what one claims to believe) vs. values in action (how one actually behaves). Jehovah's Witnesses often live by keeping two sets of books. One set with what they say they believe and another set with actions that are more convenient, strategic or self-serving but not necessarily in line with their espoused beliefs.

A worldly woman on our new street (Roehampton) invited me to a birthday party for her son. Mom decided she would not deny me this bit of fun, despite the fact that Jehovah's Witnesses are not supposed to celebrate their own or anyone else's birthday. She went against her own espoused beliefs, purchased and wrapped a present for the little boy, dressed me up in a cute outfit, and sent me off to the birthday party a few doors away.

I recall walking to the door carrying the present and feeling distinctly uncomfortable - as if I was doing something wrong. I was shy and combined with the creeping feeling of discomfort about doing something wrong, I could not bring myself to ring the doorbell. I returned home. I did not even allow myself to leave the present at the door. I'll never know exactly what was going on in my little mind, but it seems I had already absorbed an internal interdiction against going to birthday parties - even though my mother was willing to go against the organization's rule and let me go this one time. The organization had, at this pre-school age, imposed their beliefs in my head. Already, Watchtower's

(Jehovah's) instructions superseded my mother's direct permission. Of course, it made Mom proud, as she interpreted it, that I chose to obey Jehovah first.

That was my first experience with the inevitable inner conflict any child in a high-control cult experiences – the desire to participate in life - which conflicts with implanted interdictions against any participation in life in "*the world*". It was a constant inner push/pull. The heart and mind naturally giving inner consent to completely normal desires, but then having the energy of normal inner consent blocked by indoctrinated fears of breaking an expectation of some higher power. The natural impulses saying "Yes!" and reaching toward what seemed like life-enhancing activities, with an indoctrinated, foreign-sourced conscience saying "No!" and pulling back. Caught in such a crazy-making inner dialectic, how could a child of this high-control group not grow up full of repressive, neurotic tendencies?

CHAPTER 7

Vancouver, British Columbia

When I was almost six my father decided to pack up the three of us and move twenty-five hundred miles from Toronto to The Yukon. The Yukon!? (The Yukon is a Territory in remote, northwest Canada – to the north of the province of British Columbia and beside the state of Alaska.) Who knows what my father intended to do there. Perhaps he had not heard the gold rush was over and he wanted to pan for gold. My mother wanted to pan for converts in Toronto not in the far north, but somehow Dad talked her into a move to another distant, remote location.

Dad purchased a pickup truck and outfitted it with a cabin over the cargo area. He prepared this truck for our move to the Yukon, but before we headed northwest, we went southeast to the International Convention of Jehovah's Witnesses being held in New York City in the summer of 1953. My mother's brothers and sisters and their families went too and we all camped together for the eight days (yes, eight long days!) of the convention in the large "tent/trailer city" constructed for many thousands of the delegates. Dad had placed a mattress on top of the luggage in the cargo part of the truck and my parents slept there. A bed was made for me on the bench seat of the cab. I did not relish any part of this dusty camping experience, particularly using public washrooms as bathing and toilet facilities. Loud-speakers broadcast talks coming in from Yankee Stadium so delegates who were camping did not have to try and make their way into the depths of New York City to receive their *"spiritual food"*. I was barely five, but I could not wait for that convention to end and for it to be just Mom, Dad and I travelling back home.

Once home, my parents began packing up the bare essentials we would take with us on our move to the Yukon Territories. That trip west in November of 1953 is one of my favorite family memories. I sat nestled between the two people I loved most on the planet and enjoyed a sweet sense of security. I again slept on the bench seat in the cab of the truck and had the most amazing view each night through the windshield, of the expanse of millions of stars. While I felt so central and important sitting between my mother and father as we drove west, at night gazing up at the stars, it was abundantly clear that I was nothing but a speck of dust in this immense universe.

We never made it to The Yukon. For some reason we took a detour and ended up in Vancouver, British Columbia where my sister was born. But for a while my mother and I stayed in Edmonton, Alberta while my father pressed on to Vancouver alone. My mother worked as a domestic for a high-powered couple and since we would only be in Edmonton for a short time, I did not go to school. I spent entire winter days skating on an outdoor rink built for the high rise. Mom could not get me off of that skating rink. I was consumed by propelling my little body across the vast expanse of ice on dull blades. Now I have two granddaughters who glide across the ice as elite competitive skaters, one competing in dance and the other competing in both singles and pairs categories. She not only glides across the ice, but flies through the air being thrown by her partner for twists and jumps. Sometimes dreams of little girls do come true. It just might take a generation or two.

Once all together again as a family in Vancouver, my parents rented a big old Victorian house on Jervis Street, one block from the beach (Pacific Ocean) and Vancouver's Stanley Park. We lived on the main floor of the house and my parents let out the rooms on the two floors above. Dad worked as a mechanic in a garage nearby.

I have no recollection of going to meetings or going in service with my mother at this time. If I did, which I assume I did, it made no conscious impression on me. I do recall during that period visiting at the home of former JW *"Gilead"* missionaries who were in our congregation. (Gilead was a Watchtower school for training missionaries that were sent to foreign assignments after their training.) My best recollection is that this couple had served in New Zealand. While my mother listened to their stories of devoted missionary work somewhere in the South Seas, I was in the dimly lit basement with their twelve year old son, who did his best to explore my six year old southerly regions. I only told my mother about the molestation or experimentation years later. As a child I knew something was wrong but did not want to create a problem for the boy, myself or our families by reporting it. It all seemed so bizarre - like a bad dream. Unfortunately, there would be more unsavory, abusive, anxiety-producing situations like that, experienced as a Jehovah's Witness child and teenager.

After we'd been in Vancouver about a year and a half, my father was now ready to pack up and move back to Toronto for some other job opportunity. For some reason my mother, the new baby and I would not accompany him right away. He parked Mom, the baby and me in a tiny, two-room, wood shack on Hardwick Street, in Burnaby, B.C. It was not just a shack made *of* wood, but a shack originally made *for* wood – for the storage of wood, not for the housing of humans. I guess that would make it more accurately a woodshed not a wood shack!

My mother's Jehovah's Witness, widow, Aunt Clara (my mother was named after her) lived across the street from this shack with her two almost adult children, Ruth and David. My mother's Aunt was a chiropractor. Her home was a nice little house, as were most of the homes on the street. One day when a little boy walked me home from school, I went and sat on the steps of my great Aunt Clara's house so the boy would think I lived in that normal house and not in the dilapidated woodshed that was actually our home. My mother saw my ruse and must have felt bad, but she never called me on it. Perhaps she understood that I was just trying to create another good impression.

Behind the houses on our side of Hardwick Street there were woods carpeted with large, lush ferns. My mother's cousin, Ruth (she must have been about seventeen at that time) would take me (about seven) out into the woods and find a warm, dry spot for us to sit amidst the ferns. She would then read a chapter of the Lucy Maud Montgomery book, "*Anne of Green Gables*". Chinks of sunlight bathed us with warmth and Ruth's voice purred out the drama and comedy of a little orphan girl's life in rural Prince Edward Island. Ruth's then deceased father was British and Ruth had acquired a slight

English accent from him. It made her readings all the more captivating. What a delicious memory!

That was my first really memorable experience enjoying non-Witness literature. How I looked forward to each weekly installment of *Anne of Green Gables*. The majority of books that I can recall in our home were all published by the WBTS -- hardly designed to engage the curious, fanciful mind of a growing girl. Thank you cousin Ruth for choosing to read *Anne of Green Gables* rather than Bible stories. I treasure the memory of you, the glorious, green beds of ferns and the delightful dilemmas of that iconic, little red-headed girl named "*Anne Shirley*".

On Hardwick St with Great Aunt Clara and Cousin Ruth's house behind me, in Burnaby, British Columbia. I am holding a neighbor's little dog in my arms.

A couple of years later I was able to read other secular books for children such as "*The Five Little Peppers and How They Grew*", "*Black Beauty*", "*Huckleberry Finn*" and "*Little Women*" and basked in the warm glow of normal (albeit fictional) lives, exciting challenges and happy endings. There are few things that excite me more than a good book – as the book-lined walls in our home attest. However, it was while sitting enveloped by soft, green ferns in the woods of Burnaby, B.C., listening to my cousin read "*Anne of Green Gables*", that I had my first real taste of the wonders, insights, options and pleasures available to me in books.

Every story is us.
~Rumi

CHAPTER 8

Accessory to a Crime

In Burnaby I spent a lot of time playing at the edge of the woods behind our shack. Using large, fallen, rotting tree trunks I created an imaginary home and fashioned play things from whatever I could find in the woods, to decorate my little house. I recall humming a song popular at the time, called "*The Wayward Wind*". The lyrics were about a "*restless wind that yearned to wander*". I thought I just liked the song, but reading the lyrics now, I see I must have been a lonely little girl pining for her ever-absent father: "*In a lonely shack by a railroad track, I spent my younger days ... And I was born, the next of kin, the next of kin to the wayward wind.*" Written just for me!

Now, I know that, as a sensitive child, I was not only using the song to express my longing for my father, but I was probably expressing some of my mother's pain about the wayward, wandering ways of her husband. It is not my sense that he was wayward with other women, but rather more literally in his ever-present yen to wander back and forth across the country. But ... who knows? If my mother ever suspected my father had philandering ways, she never said so to me.

Many years later it was confirmed in my own therapy that I had absorbed and carried a lot of the pain of my parents. It then became my task to release the pain that was not really mine to bear - especially my father's pain. There would be enough of my own pain, from being caught in a controlling cult, to work through later.

While living in the *"lonely shack"* on Hardwick Street, we had an unexpected visitor - a woman named Colleen who had lived with her husband in the rooming house my mother ran back in Vancouver. My father and mother had become friendly with this couple, Colleen and Johnny (not their real names) while they roomed in our house.

Now, a year or so later, Colleen had come alone to see my mother and the two of them spoke in clipped, urgent-sounding whispers. I was perplexed about what was going on, especially because my mother suddenly looked very serious. Popping in and out of the house from playing with my friends, I picked up snippets of their conversations but still could not figure out what was really going on – I just knew it wasn't good. Gaps in my memory and understanding were filled in years later by my mother who recounted the whole story to my sister and myself as adults. The scenario Mom told us, went like this:

Colleen's husband, Johnny, had fallen in with a group of unsavory friends who proposed a way they could all get their hands on some fast money. Johnny, having trouble finding a job at the time, allowed himself to be talked into participating in the robbery of a jewelry store. He never dreamed, naively, that things could escalate to something more than a robbery. He later claimed he did not know one of his partners in crime would be carrying a gun. When the police arrived at the scene of the jewelry store, just as the thieves were leaving with their heist, the robber with the gun, shot and fatally wounded, one of the policemen. The thieves then escaped in their get-away-car.

Now my Jehovah's Witness mother was harboring the wife of a man being sought by the police for murder. (If a murder is committed during a crime in Canada, everyone involved is charged with the murder, not just the one who had the gun and pulled the trigger.)

Mom could not find it in her heart to turn this terrified, crying woman out of our house. With Colleen sitting at our table sobbing and wondering aloud if she would ever reunite with her husband Johnny, Mom was now linked to a murder investigation. Colleen would be high on the list of people the police would want to interrogate with respect to the robbery and murder of a fellow policeman. There was Mom – a law-abiding Jehovah's Witness caught up sheltering a key witness in a robbery-cum-murder case.

A variety of frightening scenarios about what could happen next were running through Mom's mind. She was thinking about how if her involvement in this crime, however remote, became known, or worse yet the robbery gang showed up at our house to pick up Colleen, it would bring reproach on Jehovah's name and his organization! Mom must have also been concerned about the danger she and her two little ones would be in if the gang showed up on our doorstep.

Johnny, right after the robbery and shooting, had somehow contacted his wife and told her to find Clara and see if she could stay with her. Of course, neither Johnny nor his wife, in their preoccupation with their own exploding crisis, thought of the terrible position in which they were placing my mother. My father, now in Toronto, could be of no help to my mother. Sadly, this was nothing new for Mom.

Another of my mother's fears was that this Johnny guy would show up wanting to hide out in our house, or ... that he would show up to fetch his wife and the police would arrive on his tail. As it turned out, Mom was right to be afraid. Johnny did show up at our shack – alone fortunately. I do recall all of us sitting at our table as he pulled a dark velvet, cloth pouch out of his pocket. He spilled the contents of the pouch onto the table. Shiny rings of all sizes sparkled before us and Johnny said we could each choose any one we wanted. As I reached for one with a turquoise gem stone, my mother pulled back my hand, and - shaking - told Johnny in no uncertain terms that neither she nor her child would accept any of his stolen merchandise. She stated that she wanted them both to leave before they involved her anymore in this whole terrible affair. They soon gathered their things and left - to my mother's relief.

Johnny was eventually caught and stood trial with his cohorts for robbery and the murder of a policeman. He was sentenced to several years in prison. My parents ever heard from, or about, Colleen or Johnny again.

Looking back I marvel at how my mother handled that situation. She was proudly known among all the residents of Hardwick Street as a Jehovah's Witness and she must have been terrified that the police would converge around our home. Now THAT would not reflect well on the organization or Jehovah's name. THAT would not leave the good impression she so cultivated. She could have turned Colleen away the moment she understood the full implications of her visit, but she did not. She sheltered her for a night while they tried to figure out Colleen's options. Mom was put in a real double-bind and handled the whole situation pretty well considering all the possible implications and outcomes. Fortunately, we and her beloved Watchtower organization emerged unscathed by the whole episode.

Mother, as a few of these stories about her illustrate, was often of two minds. With her mind she seemed to believe and follow the Jehovah's Witness doctrines to the letter. Yet, when she found herself in situations that were not black and white and where the organization's answers for everything did not seem to work or apply, she allowed her heart and her basic human goodness to govern – as in the above situation. The famous child pediatrician and psychoanalyst, D. W. Winnicott said: "*I would rather be the child of a mother who has all the inner conflicts of the human being than be mothered by someone for whom all is easy and smooth, who knows all the answers, and is a stranger to doubt.*" Unfortunately, it was usually the indoctrinated JW mother, having all the Watchtower's answers, who won the internal conflict in my Mom's mind. But I have great respect for her ability to step outside of the confines of JW thinking and make reasoned, independent decisions when caught in challenging circumstances.

Shortly after the nefarious events on Hardwick Street, my father must have found a place for us to live in Toronto and summoned my mother to come. So the three of us packed up and took the train three thousand miles back across Canada to reunite with him in Toronto. Mom was again on her own to cope with two young children day and night on this four day train trip across the continent. I never heard her complain. My sister was a baby in diapers. There were no disposable diapers and baby wipes back then. I just can't imagine how she coped with it all alone. For my part, sensing how difficult my mother's life was, I determined that the best way to help her was to be as good, obedient and helpful as I could. That inclination to accommodate and co-operate set me up as easy prey for upcoming religious indoctrination.

Now nearly nine years of age and back in Toronto, my life became more actively involved with the Jehovah's Witnesses. Once firmly entrenched, it would take years and much tortuous inner struggle to extricate myself. But I'm again jumping ahead in the story.

*Mom, being her 'crazy', spontaneous self the day she and her two girls arrived
back in Toronto from Burnaby, B.C, to reunite with Dad.
Dedicated Witness or not, Mom always made life, even when difficult, a lot of fun.*

CHAPTER 9

Mount Pleasant Congregation

The living-quarters in Toronto, that my Father had waiting for us, were in the partially-finished, dark basement of his boss' house in the borough of North York. Far from a palace, but better than the wood shack on Hardwick Street. I never heard my mother complain about what my father provided. She was always just happy to be with the man she loved, and now happy to be in a place less remote than Burnaby and where she could be even more actively involved in the activities of the Jehovah's Witnesses. About a year later we moved out of those basement quarters into a tiny apartment at the back of a drugstore on Avenue Road. The backyard was a gravel parking lot for the stores on Avenue Road. Rarely, if ever, did I bring school friends or even Witness friends to any of our homes. There was always the anxiety that kids from normal middle class environments would discover where and how we lived. I never wanted anyone to feel sorry for me. How we lived always seemed to be an ongoing source of embarrassment for my developing ego.

In North York we found ourselves assigned to the Mount Pleasant congregation of Jehovah's Witnesses, so named because the Kingdom Hall was situated on Mount Pleasant Road and directly across from the Mount Pleasant Cemetery. There were many brothers and sisters in this congregation that my mother already knew from when she previously lived in Toronto. So my mother, little sister and I settled comfortably into all the Witness activities. Those activities included 5 hours of meetings each week and a goal of going in the door-to-door preaching work for at least a couple of hours each week. I would accompany my mother in field service on the weekends. She regularly went out with other sisters during the week as well.

There were three girls and one boy around my age in the Mount Pleasant congregation: Belinda, Carole, Marilyn and Bobby (their real names). During the intermission between the two Sunday meetings the five of us would cross Mount Pleasant Road and go to a small corner store. Whichever one of us had any money would buy loose, penny candy and share it with the others.

I was occasionally invited to the girl's homes for lunch after Saturday's door-to-door service and got to stay, hang out and play for the afternoon. Since we girls did not have play dates with Bobby, he remained a bit of a mystery to us. Bobby was pale, blond and on the chubby side. He had no father accompany him to the Kingdom Hall. We had that in common, although I learned he had no father at home either. Bobby was not included in the girls' get-togethers but we all enjoyed his company at the Kingdom Hall. I loved our little routine of visiting the corner store during breaks between the meetings. We'd stand outside the store to eat the candy while Bobby made we four girls giggle with his hokey jokes and silly antics. For a few minutes each Sunday, Bobby had a captive audience and he gave us his version of a mini stand-up comedy routine ... and we loved him for it.

One Sunday we arrived at the Kingdom Hall expecting to continue our Sunday meeting routine (kiddy candy break and comedy routine included) only to get the wide-eyed, whispered news that ten year old Bobby had died the night before.

It was explained to us that in the midst of an epileptic seizure Bobby had swallowed his tongue, cutting off his airway, and died. My nine year old mind could not comprehend. How could this be? Someone must be playing an awful joke. I just knew it was a joke – and one I did not like. Bobby could NOT be dead. Please Jehovah, our friend CANNOT be dead!

At the meetings we had always been told, and believed, that we would be among millions who would never die because we would survive the Battle of Armageddon when Jehovah destroyed the wicked. We would then live forever on a paradise earth. (JWs believe only a select few humans will go to heaven. The rest, called *"the great crowd of other sheep"*, will receive their reward of everlasting life on a paradise Earth.) It never occurred to me that any of we Witnesses would die before Armageddon. Never! Not once! Not my mother. Not the brothers and sisters. Not my young friends. Not me. We were going to live forever. That was Jehovah's plan. That was His promise. Why even Mommy said so! I was a real little '*true believer*' and Bobby's death just did not compute with my naive, black-and-white, unquestioning, gullible, indoctrinated understanding of things.

We went home from the Kingdom Hall in shock. Hours passed. No one called to say it was all a terrible mistake. A day passed and I had to try to admit to myself that perhaps my friend's death was not just a bad joke. His death was truly an existential shock to my young nervous system. Bobby's death brought everything I knew and counted on, even as a nine year old, into question.

Imagine the psychological implications of believing from a young age that you will never die - that you are exempt from the fate of the rest of humankind simply by virtue of your connection to the Watchtower Society. What a complete distortion of the natural order of things, and yet the perfect carrot on a stick to have people (including little people) believe and follow your religion. Bobby's death just did not gel with my world view of all Jehovah's Witnesses surviving Armageddon and living forever in paradise. The Watchtower indoctrination had imparted some feeling of existential invulnerability to me. Now, if death could claim a young person in the congregation right on the cusp of Armageddon, what other unexpected dangers could pop up and afflict us? How safe were we, really? What or who would be next? Was there anything we could truly depend on? My immature, manufactured faith was shaken.

Of course, I was just a nine year old and very naive. With the sudden death of Bobby, a great deal of my comfort and sense of protection in life and in the Jehovah's Witness organization began to evaporate. Could I really trust Jehovah or the Watchtower Society? Could I trust that my mother really knew what she was doing by aligning herself with them?

Shortly before Bobby's death, his single mother Bessie Penny, had married a brother named Charlie Martin (their real names). After her marriage Bessie did something which caused a lot of talk in the congregation. She kept her own name (how avant-garde!) so that she would still have the same surname as her son – "*Penny*". Such a choice was quite unheard of back then.

At the funeral home, Bessie Penny's pain was palpable. I had never seen anyone in a state of abject grief. Bessie Penny looked like a grey, stone statue staring right through anyone who approached her. My mother quietly suggested we children not speak to Bessie, as seeing Bobby's friends might just be too much for her to bear. The casket was open. Bobby looked like he was sleeping. He had always looked pale, but now ... I had never seen a dead body and certainly not one of a vital young person about the same age as myself. It was all so surreal. I was still secretly hoping it was a bad joke and that Mommy would pull me aside with an explanation that would finally make sense. Maybe Bobby would sit up and yell *"Just kidding!"* - *"Just a joke, folks!"*. Neither happened. I remained confused, fearful and shaken to the core.

A couple of weeks after Bobby's funeral and burial, Bessie Penny informally announced to the brothers and sisters at the Mount Pleasant Kingdom Hall that she would drop the surname, *Penny* and take her husband's last name, *Martin*. At the same time she changed her commonly-used forename from *Bessie*, to her full given name, *Elizabeth*. The message went out through the congregation that now that Bobby was dead, we were never to call her *Bessie Penny* again. She would now only be known as, and respond to, *"Elizabeth Martin"*. This name change seemed, to me, like the final nail in Bobby Penny's coffin. All tangible traces of Bobby and links to him seemed severed with that name change. The brothers had assured us that the memory of Bobby was with Jehovah and that during the thousand year reign of Christ, Bobby Penny would be resurrected from the dead to live on a paradise earth with his mother. But, I worried, he would arise from his grave, be looking for his mother, *"Bessie Penny"* and not be able to find her. She had abandoned that name for the new name, *"Elizabeth Martin"*! I found this disturbing. How would Bobby ever find her? How would he know to ask for *"Elizabeth Martin"*?

Imagining Bobby's plight upon his resurrection brought up all kinds of seemingly unanswerable questions in my young mind, but we were not allowed to ask questions at the meetings. Questions that raised the specter of death and its attendant anxiety were carefully avoided by the Watchtower Society – unless they were speaking of the destruction of the wicked at Armageddon. They offered their adepts beautiful, pre-packaged guarantees about how some obedient followers of Jehovah and his organization would reign on thrones in heaven while others would live forever on a paradise Earth. In fact, it was generally not viewed well if you asked any questions about any of their doctrines, promises or pronouncements. We were simply to receive and regurgitate the information as dispensed from the Society's literature and talks. At a very young age I learned that at the Kingdom Hall I was expected to keep my questions to myself, my mouth shut. However, suppressed questions fester and percolate and eventually jump out demanding answers. While waiting for the time and place to ask my questions, the unanswered questions bore holes in my newly failing foundation of faith.

Weeks after Bobby's death, I continued to ruminate about what would happen when he was finally resurrected and searched for his mother Bessie Penny. No Bessie Penny would be found. Bessy Penny had also been laid to rest and had resurrected herself as Elizabeth Martin. Would mother and son ever find each other and be reunited? As with all imponderables, my mother assured me that *"Jehovah would take care of it"*. My pre-teen self did not feel reassured.

When no Biblical or JW publication explications for problems came to mind, my mother would always rely on the Watchtower provided explanation that *"Jehovah would provide"* - the answer, the resources, the protection, the understanding - whatever his servants needed. The provisions would not always be made precisely when we wanted them or in the exact way we wanted them, but if we would just *"wait on Jehovah"* they would come. Answers like that seemed designed to shut one down. Cult experts call such oft-used phrases *"thought-stopping"* language. 'Thought-stoppers', such as *"Wait on Jehovah"* never succeeded in stopping my young mind. Perhaps all my questions and ruminations were an unconscious defense (keeping me mentally busy and preoccupied) against newly awakened death anxiety. Whatever the case, Bobby's death had opened the door to serious anxiety which, in turn, provoked newfound doubts.

"Extraordinary claims require extraordinary evidence." ~Carl Sagan

A few months after Bobby Penny's untimely death I began to have a recurring nightmare:

> *I am standing alone waiting at the corner of Avenue Road and Lawrence Avenue for our regular ride, with an elder, to the meeting at the Mount Pleasant Kingdom Hall. I see the car, and the brother driving it, approach. He pulls over. I open the door and get into the passenger seat. We seem, at first, to be driving the usual route to the Kingdom Hall but suddenly none of the predictable points of reference are visible. We are no longer*

taking the usual road to the Kingdom Hall. We seem to have moved onto a highway. I look over at the elder to ask where we are going, only to discover that it is no longer the elder driving the vehicle. It is now an unrecognizable, dark, shadowy figure in the driver's seat. I freeze with fear and grip the arm rest on the car door. No words are spoken. The shadowy figure stops the vehicle and we get out and walk to the middle of an open field. The figure is still shrouded in darkness and signals me to move closer to a large tree-stump. I somehow know that the dark figure expects me to put a leg across the tree stump. I do. The shrouded figure now has an axe in its hands and raises the axe above its head in order to swing it down and chop off my leg. I awaken just before the axe hits my leg.

It was a terrifying dream and once awake from it, I was always afraid to go back to sleep in case it would resume. I did not have the dream every night, but it recurred in exactly the same way for months.

As a child I interpreted the dream literally, assuming it was about being kidnapped and harmed by a stranger – as we were often warned about by teachers and parents. In later years, once studying psychology, I interpreted the dream as being about a deep-seated fear of losing my often absent, and seemingly unknowable father – as if losing him would be like losing a pillar of my life and then only being able to limp through the rest of life without him.

Now, with more knowledge and experience under my belt I know the dream was about the effect of Bobby Penny's death on my young, indoctrinated world view. In the dream I am trying to follow the established pattern of going along with the brothers (an elder) to the place (the Kingdom Hall) where I would receive the regular JW indoctrination. I am not the driving force in my life, but a Jehovah's Witness elder is driving me through the scene. Suddenly the brother/elder I trust to drive the vehicle (of my life) morphs into a dark, shrouded figure. This new 'entity' forces a change of direction upon me (onto a 'higher way') and is about to force me to have a leg (a central pillar of my life) severed. Since legs are what we *stand* on, I interpret that the shadowy, specter of death was slicing away my JW *understand*ing of life and the future. With a leg removed by the dark, shadowy figure, I would not be able to *stand* on the fantasy premises (or promises) of the Kingdom Hall. The shadow of death slid into my life and threatened to sever the JW-imposed indoctrination and invalid under*stand*ing. With death inserting its presence into my life, JW fantasy promises no longer had 'a leg to stand on'.

With that nightmare, my subconscious was telling me that the reality of Bobby's death put at risk my understanding of life and how it would unfold, as interpreted for me by my mother, the brothers, the talks and literature at the Kingdom Hall. The harsh reality of death helped expose, loosen and begin to remove the erroneous understanding, freeing me to begin to construct a life based on a more accurate understanding of the realities of existence.

This dream, terrifying as it was, was a gift from my subconscious. It was so powerful that it could not easily be forgotten and lurked for decades at the periphery of my consciousness waiting for me to finally 'get' its full meaning. Sometimes loss acts as a prompt, forcing us to take an axe to our current understanding of life.

With a more mature, informed interpretation of that dream I am able to see that when I was about nine years old an unexpected confrontation with the reality of death forced a serious look (albeit a mainly subconscious one) at how I was moving through life and at what informed my understanding of it. The anxiety awakened by the death of Bobby Penny, set in motion a more reasoned, accurate view of the world for little indoctrinated me. Though at times terrifying, the new understanding that we are not special, are not protected, and are not exempt from death by virtue of our association with the sect of Jehovah's Witnesses – once fully understood and integrated – would be ultimately liberating and life-enhancing.

...Your way begins on the other side.
Become the sky.
Take an axe to the prison wall.
Escape.
Walk out like someone suddenly born into colour.
Do it now.
You're covered with thick cloud.
Slide out the side.
Die, and be quiet.
Quietness is the surest sign that you've died.
Your old life was a frantic running from silence.
The speechless full moon comes out now.
~Rumi

CHAPTER 10

The Hows

One of the JW lawyers who represented the Watchtower Bible & Tract Society of Canada was a member of the Mount Pleasant congregation. Glen How, Q.C. (Queen's Council), and his wife Margaret, were a powerful pair both inside and outside of the congregation. Margaret was even more officious, it seemed to me, than her Rhodes Scholar husband, Glen. Perhaps I perceived her that way due to her erect posture, clipped gait, serious demeanor and formal British accent.

There were periods of time in Canada, especially in the Catholic province of Quebec, where Jehovah's Witnesses were a banned group -- banned from engaging in most of their religious activities by the Catholic Church aligned government. Feeling they must obey God not man, JWs continued to meet in clandestine ways despite the ban and continued their preaching work with the ever present risk of being arrested for so doing. (My husband, living in Montreal at that time as a young teen, went with his mother in the door-to-door service. She knew they could have been arrested but was willing to risk her son having a police record and incurring the ire of her non-Jehovah's Witness husband, in order to obey the expectations of the Watchtower Society.)

Glen How, argued cases before the provincial courts and the Supreme Court of Canada on behalf of the Jehovah's Witnesses in order to regain and protect their rights of freedom of speech (going to door-to-door), religious expression (publishing their tracts, magazines and books) and freedom of assembly (holding meetings). The cases Glen How argued and won for the Watchtower Bible & Tract Society of Canada are now recognized by the Canadian government as having paved the way for the Canadian Bill of Rights and the Canadian Charter of Rights and Freedoms. (Truth be told the Watchtower organization was never interested in helping Canadians develop their Charter of Human Rights. They were only interested in procuring their own religious freedoms. They were not averse, however, to accepting credit and accolades for helping the cause of civil rights in Canada.) Glen How was eventually awarded The Order of Canada for this contribution to the rights and freedoms of Canadians. He remained a Jehovah's Witness for the rest of his life and a legal consultant for the Watchtower organization.

I knew Glen How and his then wife, Margaret, simply as Brother and Sister How. One Saturday morning I was assigned to accompany Sister How in the door-to-door ministry. I was about nine years old at the time. At one house, when a woman opened the door, a vicious little dog rushed out onto the step and bit me on the leg. As a result of the attack my tights were torn and my leg was bleeding. Oh, oh! This did not bode well for the householder. Your dog biting a little girl in front of Margaret How, wife of eminent lawyer Glen How could, at the very least, result in a serious tongue-lashing!

Sister How immediately tore a strip off of the dog owner, telling her that the dog was a threat to the community and should be put-down. She informed the householder that her husband was a prominent lawyer and she would be consulting him about an immediate legal response to this vicious attack! I kept thinking, *"Please stop Sister How, it's not that bad! Please don't make such a scene!"*, but I said nothing out loud. One did not interrupt Sister How. Nothing ensued, of course. Sister How had the satisfaction of expressing her indignation and chastising the woman for harboring a dangerous dog - and in the end - that seemed to be enough.

Several years later, as a full-time pioneer, I found myself working as a part-time typist in legal offices shared by Glen How and lawyer, Frank Mott-Trille. I worked for Frank but was always intrigued by the fanfare and flourish that surrounded the Hows every time they entered the offices. (Margaret always accompanied her husband, seeming to work as his assistant.) I recall one time when they were marching back and forth through the corridors of the office suites talking loudly about the ghastly, cannibalistic elements of organ transplants, and how Jehovah's Witnesses had every right to refuse them on those grounds. Brother How had a distinctive voice and probably used that and his natural bombast to great effect in courtrooms defending the rights of the Watchtower Society. Glen How's skills were also central to the Watchtower's defense of cases brought before the courts by hospitals and governments trying to intervene and protect children being denied blood transfusions by their indoctrinated, misguided JW parents.

Glen How eventually ran the legal department of the Canadian Branch of the WBTS. He died in 2009. I've since been told by a former Witness, that my cousin John MacEwan (named after our grandfather) now directs the legal department set up by Glen How in the Canadian Branch Headquarters.

The original How couple (Glen remarried after Margaret's death) were kind and cordial to me and my family. They always seemed larger than life, certainly not your typical Jehovah's Witness couple, and were highly regarded by JWs across Canada.

Margaret How & Glen How posing with Fred Franz (lower right) about 15 years after the incident with Margaret, me and the dog. The only photograph I could find of Margaret How in our photograph collection.

CHAPTER 11

But Please Mommy!

Have I mentioned my youthful competitive streak? What about my childhood need to please? I know I have mentioned the need, absorbed from my mother and the Watchtower organization, to set a good example and leave a good impression. Some of those young traits must have played a role in my unexpected announcement that I wanted to be baptized at the next district assembly. I was barely eleven years old.

I doubt that dedicating my life to serve Jehovah throughout eternity was the motivation driving this big decision – especially since my little crisis of confidence in Jehovah and the Watchtower organization after Bobby died. Perhaps I just wanted to be the first eleven year old to be baptized ... in the Mount Pleasant congregation. Did my mother push me to make the decision? Not overtly, but it is possible that her immense pride in my little JW accomplishments was quietly nudging me in that direction. I have no memories of her saying I must now be baptized. I was aware, however, that it would please her immensely.

Back then there were no pre-baptism sessions with questions to answer in front of the elders. You just made the decision and then at the next assembly sat in the section of the stadium cordonned off for those wanting to be baptized. A talk was given. You publicly answered a couple of questions affirming that you had dedicated yourself to serve Jehovah God. (I do not recall any pledge of loyalty to His earthly organization, at that time.) You were then escorted to the baptismal pool, or as in my case, driven to a nearby lake. Jehovah's Witnesses believe in a complete immersion of the body in water for baptisms. Fortunately, I knew how to swim and was not afraid of being dunked under water by a brother I did not know. Well ... then again, maybe I was.

The Mount Pleasant congregation in Toronto was assigned to a District Assembly held in Ottawa, Ontario that year. Since my father did not attend conventions, we asked for a ride to the Ottawa convention with an English brother who had a prosthetic leg and drove an English-made vehicle - a Vauxhall. I had heard my mechanic father say that most English cars were *"mechanical catastrophes"*, so I was a little concerned about our safety during the two hundred mile trip. During that three hour drive from Toronto to Ottawa, my preoccupation was not about my upcoming baptism but about whether having an artificial leg could interfere with one's ability to drive a *"mechanical catastrophe"*. Apparently not, we arrived safe and sound.

My mother had arranged for us to stay in a room let out by a non-Jehovah's Witness private home owner. The Watchtower organization canvased private homes seeking people who were willing to offer rooms to let for the delegates to the assembly. Our rented room was only a few blocks away from the football stadium where the convention was being held.

I awoke the morning of the baptism feeling anxious, with a vague sense of impending doom. But at eleven years of age I had no way to precisely articulate the feeling. Mommy, while also looking after my little four year old sister, was helping me pack a towel and bathing cap in a little bag and giving me a few instructions for the day. I was wearing a white bathing suit with funny little black scribbled faces all over it, under my dress. As we walked up a hill to my death by drowning, er ... baptism, I finally worked up the courage to tell my mother that I had changed my mind. I did not want to be baptized after all. Her reply was not what I hoped for:

Mommy: *You told the brothers that you are getting baptized and that is what you will do.*
Me: *But please, Mommy ... I've changed my mind ... I'm not ready.*
Mommy: *You have been telling everyone that you are ready to be baptized for the last few months. You will not embarrass me by changing your mind now. You've committed yourself. It's too late to change your mind!*
Me: *But I'm really scared Mommy. My stomach hurts. I think I'm going to throw up!*
Mommy: *If you throw up, you throw up. There is no backing out now. That's it. No more talking about it, Bonnie. Let's go.*

So that was it. I'd made my baptismal bed, so to speak. No reprieves, even for nervous eleven year olds who thought they were ready for things they were not. I was not allowed to change my mind. That eleven year old mind could not seem to come up with any other option than to proceed as planned.

Mom was not allowed to sit with me in the section cordoned off for the baptismal candidates, besides she had my sister to look after. I sat there alone amidst mainly adults and a few older teenagers. One soon-to-be-baptized woman asked if I had been separated from my parents and was sitting in the wrong place. *"Nope, I'm the silly girl who thought she was ready to be baptized"*, I thought.

I tried to listen to the Baptism talk – as much as an eleven year old listens to any talk. The seriousness of the whole situation and ceremony suddenly seemed more frightening than ever. I wanted to bolt and run. But where could I run to? My mother had made clear that she would not welcome me. Besides, I did not know exactly where she was seated in the big stadium. She had said only that she would meet me at the lake. I felt trapped. Every muscle in my body wanted to flee. But there was no way out. No one in the stadium would understand my not wanting to dedicate my life to Jehovah. I wasn't even in my own home town, so I could not just leave and walk home. It all began to feel like a horrible punishment for claiming to be ready for something I was not.

After the talk, the baptismal candidates were ferried by buses to the baptismal site at a lake outside of Ottawa. I have no memory of the drive there. Perhaps in my distress I went numb (dissociated). As we arrived at the lake, it was evident that the body of water remained very shallow way out from the shore. JW men in bathing suits and white t-shirts were far out in the lake waiting for us to wade out to them. With a lot of anxiety and a heavy heart I walked to my death by drowning, er ... baptism, for what seemed like several minutes. Finally I got to a brother standing in water deep enough to dunk me without banging my head on the bottom of the lake. He looked surprised to see such a little girl approach him but said nothing. He made sure that I was holding my nostrils shut with my thumb and forefinger and immersed me - quickly in, quickly out.

The baptizing brother made no spiritual pronouncements before or after the immersion. There was no Universal Studios movie sound track to magnify the solemnity or import of the event. The entire event (talk and immersion) was all quite anti-climactic, mundane and spiritless. That was that. I was dunked (baptized) but nothing felt different. I had imagined I might have suddenly felt more mature, might have felt more love for, and proximity to Jehovah and might have been more strongly determined to serve him forever. But no, nothing seemed to be any different than from how I felt before the dunk.

I waded slowly back to shore and was reunited with my mother who was beaming with pride. Her daughter was one of the youngest, if not the youngest, to ever be baptized in the Mount Pleasant congregation. Big Brownie points for Mommy! What a good Christian mother she must be ... *"raising up her child in the way she should go ..."*!

Yes, I had created the good impression Mommy so craved. But at what cost? One of the immediate costs for volunteering to get baptized and then trying to back out was that I felt that I must be a bad person. Surely I must not have what the Witnesses called a *"good heart"*. A person with a good heart would never want to back out of dedicating their life to Jehovah. Someone with a good heart would want to serve Jehovah and demonstrate that intent by a public baptism as His organization expected. I felt a lot of guilt about the whole episode of wanting to change my mind. Inner conflict about my place in this religious organization and my relationship with Jehovah God would only grow and accompany me over the years.

Was I forced to be baptized? Forced? Not really. Unduly influenced? Yes. While I was the one to instigate the whole thing, it was only after being subjected to the constant indoctrination and expectations of the 'religion'. However, I was not allowed to rethink my premature, childish impulse. My mother considered it a non-negotiable commitment and would not allow me to reconsider. While I initiated the process, at the end I did feel forced into being baptized. Mom clearly did not want to endure the embarrassment of having to tell her friends that I had changed my mind and backed out. I didn't know then, but that 'not-being-allowed-to-change-my-mind-situation-without-incurring-the-anger-disapproval-and-disappointment-of-my-mother', was a bit of symbolic foreshadowing about wanting to change my mind and leave the sect and not being able to without hurting my mother ... and my life.

Now so many years later I have learned that the Watchtower organization is encouraging, or should I say unduly influencing, children to get baptized at an ever younger age. It is no longer unique to hear of eleven year olds being baptized into the Watchtower organization. *"Capture those born and raised in the sect, by getting them baptized young"*, is what I imagine must be the Governing Body's thinking. Once baptized, it seems that your life has been hijacked and the consequences for escape from Watchtower's influence are severe. Excommunication and total shunning serve as ever-present deterrents to anyone thinking of acting on any thoughts of liberating themselves.

Pressure to make an early, premature commitment to God and the organization, symbolized by total immersion in water becomes the ultimate trap into the cult. Children have no idea that they are entering into a stealth contract of loyalty to the Watchtower organization and that to dare reconsider that 'contract' in the future could and would probably incur catastrophic familial and social consequences. Joseph Goebbels, Nazi Minister of Propaganda said, "*...a sharp sword must always stand behind propaganda if it is to be really effective.*"

You are not a drop in the ocean. You are the entire ocean in a drop.
~Rumi

You are the TRUTH from foot to brow.
Now what else would you like to know?
~Rumi

CHAPTER 12

I Am ... Alive!

During this same time period I had an experience that has never left me. It stands in stark contrast to my reluctant baptism. My father had just bought me a brand new, shiny, red, two-wheel bicycle. It was the best gift ever. I was over-the-moon happy! I went everywhere on that new bike and eventually was so good at riding it that I barely knew where I stopped and the bike began. That red bike and I were one.

One gorgeous spring day I had been out alone, riding my bike, with the wind in my hair, sun on my face, sometimes with my hands on the handle bars - sometimes not. Suddenly a feeling of euphoria, of incredible well-being enveloped me ... a feeling of utter, complete aliveness ... a feeling of total freedom and oneness with everything. The well-being I experienced came from within, it had not been imposed or applied from without. I now know that I was experiencing a moment of spontaneous bliss or oneness. My body buzzed from the top of my head to the soles of my feet. My mouth whispered: "I AM .... I AM ..." My mind could not leave those seemingly incomplete utterances of pure beingness alone and tagged on the word "ALIVE" to complete the sentence: "I AM ... ALIVE!" "I AM ... ALIVE!"

Now I know the "I AM" by itself was a deep inner knowing of the pure beingness of my little existence. It was a profound moment of transcending my particular circumstances - a knowing that the real "I" that I was, was not defined by circumstances, limitations or problems. While that feeling was all-enveloping and euphoric, my senses were still highly alert and I recall even how at that moment I steered the front wheel of the bike into a dirt rut to avoid having to negotiate a steep curb. I recall exactly where I was on the street, the cross-street, the appearance of the houses situated there. It was a moment of acute awareness and pure consciousness on every level. That awareness brought a feeling of absolute joy with it. It was a pivotal, threshold experience that I tucked into my heart and have treasured ever since.

That "I AM ALIVE" experience was connected to no one and no thing. It just was. It emerged from the core of my being. It stands in glaring contrast to the dread, aloneness and discouragement experienced on the day of my baptism. There was more grace and goodness in that "I AM ... ALIVE" moment than in any ever experienced during my entire affiliation with the Watchtower organization.

Quiet friend who has come so far ...
In this uncontainable night,
Be the mystery at the crossroads of your senses,
The meaning discovered there.

And if the world has ceased to hear you,
Say to the silent earth: ***I flow****.*
To the rushing water,
Speak: ***I am****.*
~Rainer Maria Rilke

Yes, it took another twenty-some years for me to really claim that delicious aliveness, to claim my life as my own and exit the cult that squashes all joyful vitality and individuality. I still had to negotiate the teenage years as a reluctant Witness of Jehovah and as you probably know, it is not easy to be a teenager while a member of this totalistic, authoritarian cult.

The world is mud-luscious and puddle-wonderful.
~e.e. cummings

CHAPTER 13

Book Study Conductor

Before I was baptized I was already making prepared comments at the meetings in answer to questions in the Watchtower Magazine we were studying that week. I had also begun to 'present' the Watchtower and Awake! Magazines from door to door in the field ministry and joined the Kingdom Ministry School (the youngest to do so in that congregation at the time) giving the kind of talks that sisters are allowed to give in JW congregations. Female Witnesses are not allowed to teach males, so any time they have an assignment on the platform they have to do so by addressing another female who goes up on the platform with them. These talks by sisters were called "*demonstrations*".

It seemed I was good at presenting little demonstrations in front of small audiences in the second school and received a lot of praise for my delivery of them. The real reward was always the look of pride on my mother's face. Her life was hard and I loved bringing some happiness her way with my 'performances' at the Kingdom Hall.

Mom was a natural teacher and could have been an effective high school teacher or university professor. Instead she used her intellect, curiosity and teaching skills conducting studies with householders who were interested in the Bible, delivering talks (demonstrations) from the platform and giving comments at the Kingdom Hall. Mom was always reading the Bible and studying the Watchtower literature whenever she could. She was not reading the Bible as some sort of pious ritual or for comfort. She studied to really understand – and she did – mainly in terms of Jehovah's Witness interpretations, that is.

When the "*Aid to Understanding*" encyclopedia-like tome was released (now unavailable through JW.ORG because it was authored by supposed apostate Raymond Franz), my mother studied it in depth. It seemed to me she always had her nose in that book. I wondered if she ever came upon some of the discrepancies in the Watchtower's calculations about 1914 as the beginning of God's Kingdom rule. (Perhaps, I like to imagine, Raymond Franz had left little, hidden clues about Watchtower mistakes, discrepancies or deceits.)

Even though I admired my mother's studious devotion, it did not prompt me to want to limit my curiosity and energies to the publications of the Watchtower Bible & Tract Society for the rest of my life. Even at a young age, I had had enough of the Watchtower's teachings and was itching to learn about new things, to discover new horizons. There had to be more out there ... surely. Eventually when I got to high school, some new horizons, especially in terms of access to new information, opened up to me.

Mom was also one of the few witnesses I knew who loved knocking on peoples' doors with the aim of trying to convert any who expressed interest in the Watchtower's message. She often made the time we spent together in service more interesting by telling me the names of all the different shrubs, trees, flowers and birds as we walked between doors. Mom always did something fun or a little 'off-beat' to make service bearable for me. Sometimes she would echo back a bird's cry and I was impressed by her talent at whistling and mimicry. Even now when I hear a certain bird's song it reminds me of her and occasionally I allow myself to imagine it is my mother reaching out to connect with me. Strange the silly, little fantasy things we do to try and comfort ourselves.

One day I opened up to her and told her how difficult I found it to speak to strangers in the door-to-door work. She advised me to pretend I was a telephone pole that could talk. Huh? Looking back on that statement now, I am torn between thinking she was actually suggesting I go numb and dissociate, *or* she was suggesting that my thoughts were the cause of my anxiety and that I should just stop thinking. Who knows? Either interpretation of her suggestion makes it an inappropriate one.

Once when Mom was making a return visit to a householder who previously expressed interest, the woman said she did not have time to talk because she was washing the floor. My mother replied, "*Well let me help you wash the floor, and then we'll sit down and talk for five minutes!*" When the woman responded that she couldn't possibly let my mother wash her dirty floor my mother said, "*Of course you can! I don't mind a bit!*" I was with her but did not join in the floor washing and stood awkwardly by the door watching my mother and this woman on hands and knees washing the floor. I was mortified with embarrassment. The woman, too, seemed uncomfortable. But my wily mother got her five minutes to witness and considered the time spent washing the floor worth it! Back then, in spite of my embarrassment, I still admired my mother so much that I did not allow myself to see what a manipulative tactic that floor washing was.

Mom also had this little trick where, as she noticed a householder's interest waning or saw them begin to slowly close the door, she would do the opposite of what people say Jehovah's Witnesses do – "*stick their foot in your door*". Instead, she would begin to slowly back up, put the magazines she was offering back in her bag, or close her Bible, all the while continuing to give her sermon in the most non-threatening way. The person at the door, being pleased to see indications that she was leaving, would relax and listen to what she had to say, believing they were finally hearing her parting words. She was extremely personable and many people ended up hearing her whole 'pitch', even saying she was welcome to return. Mom was not only a natural teacher, she was a savvy salesperson. Did she realize many of her ploys were manipulative sales techniques? I don't think she would ever have allowed herself to frame them that way. She thought she was just being clever - clever in service of truth and Jehovah.

A story told by my mother was about being out in service and walking up a long, winding, tree-lined driveway to a house in the country. Half way up the driveway, a male voice yelled: "*Stop where ya are lady. I'm standing here naked in my outdoor shower!*" My mother's cheeky reply was: "*Well, put some clothes on, I have some good news to share with you!*" (The poor man probably thought he had won the lottery or was about to receive notice of an inheritance.) She waited for a while and then yelled again, "*Are you decent? I'm headed up the drive.*" I don't recall how the scene unfolded from there but have little doubt that my mother got to deliver her disappointing "*good news*". The man must have been fully clothed because my mother would certainly not have left out that part of the story!

Mom's amazing knowledge of the Scriptures and the publications led to her interim appointment to conduct a weekly Book Study Meeting when no available brothers were deemed qualified. They must have been really desperate to allow a woman to lead a meeting in Toronto. The brothers who would have normally qualified to lead the Book Study were possibly on *"probation"* for some sort of *"conduct unbecoming a Christian"*. Making her appointment even more unusual, the Book Study was conducted in the home of the brother who had previously led the meeting. To his credit he attended every meeting Mom led and treated my mother with respect. Mom wore a little hat to signal that she knew her 'place' - subject to the brothers in attendance. She led that book study meeting for over a year. We were then studying the dense and incomprehensible *"Babylon the Great Has Fallen! God's Kingdom Rules!"* book, authored everyone believed, by Fred Franz. I loved the irony that this male-dominated, misogynist organization found themselves in a position where they had no other choice but to appoint the most qualified person available to a ministerial position - and that person was a woman! Mom did not seem to have a prideful or competitive attitude about her appointment to conduct meetings - in fact she was almost embarrassed by it. It was the budding feminist in me that secretly thought, *"Way to go, Mom!!"*

You must ask for what you really want.
Don't go back to sleep.
The door is round and open.
Don't go back to sleep.
~Rumi

CHAPTER 14

A False Self

The old Smokey Robinson hit, "*You've Really Got a Hold on Me*" is a good way to describe my relationship to the Watchtower as a teenager. I wanted to leave – didn't "*want to stay another day*", but I hadn't the foggiest idea of how a teenager could leave "*the truth*", a.k.a. her mother's precious religion.

There were so many questions and so many doubts that I had to suppress. As a teen I hated having to knock on doors peddling the Watchtower and Awake! Magazines. My body did not want to stand at the threshold of someone else's door to tell them that what they believed and held sacred was wrong. As well, I often felt a strong physical discomfort sitting in the meetings. I know now that the discomfort was my body trying to tell me what my mind was too afraid to admit. I wanted to bolt away from the Kingdom Hall and the organization. But how? It seemed impossible. They really did "*have a hold on me*". So much so that I would not even allow myself to consciously dwell on any idea of another way of life, of anything different for myself in the future.

Some part of me decided that if I was stuck as a Witness, I was not going to let anyone know that I felt stuck. I could not tolerate the thought of anyone pitying me because I was a Jehovah's Witness (probably because I already pitied myself enough for being one). So at some point I decided there was no option but to pretend I wanted nothing more than to go to meetings and door-to-door. I would act like it was just fine with me that I might have to sacrifice my life by refusing a blood transfusion. I would be the best darn teenage Witness you could find. While acting as if I was a good Witness was a psychological defense that was probably a better choice than becoming morose, depressed, or suicidal, it had another unanticipated effect. It caused me to become distanced and disconnected from my real self. It caused me to know the lonely, barren state of inauthenticity. There was no way to be honest about my deepest thoughts and feelings. My true self, my true needs had to be hidden away. Although I could never have actually identified the process then, it is abundantly clear to me now that I sacrificed my true self for a false self that could survive in the sect. I know I was not alone in such a desperate manoeuver. Shannon L. Alder says, *"One of the greatest regrets in life is being what others want you to be, rather than being yourself."*

Teacher and author, Brené Brown in her book "The Gifts of Imperfection: Let Go of Who You Think You're Supposed to Be and Embrace Who You Are", says: *"Authenticity is a collection of choices that we have to make every day. It's about the choice to show up and be real. The choice to be honest. The choice to let our true selves be seen."* Jehovah's Witnesses quickly learn that they cannot *"show up and be real"*. They learn to bury their real desires and feelings and mold themselves into the image of what a good servant of Jehovah is expected to be. In The Watchtower of Jan. 15, 1983, (p. 22), Jehovah's Witnesses were admonished to *"avoid independent thinking ... questioning the counsel that is provided by God's visible organization"* Children and teenagers in the Jehovah's Witness organization soon learn there is no place for their honesty, no place for their curiosity or questions, no place for them to be authentic and strive for normal adult independence. The tragedy is that they then grow up not knowing who they are – having lost connection with their individual, independent identity. This, to my mind, constitutes a serious form of abuse.

D. W. Winnicott, the father of child psychology was the first to speak of the true self as a sense of self based on the spontaneous, authentic experiences of aliveness in a child. My experience on the bicycle, for example, was a rare moment of authentic, spontaneous aliveness and connection with my true self. Winnicott described how children can easily build a false self and a defensive facade housed behind an appearance or imitation of being real. He described how easily a child's spontaneity can be crushed because of the need for compliance with unrealistic, outside expectations, usually the parents' (or parental substitutes such as a religion). It is in the false self, says Winnicott that *"Other people's expectations can become of overriding importance, overlaying or contradicting the original sense of self, the one connected to the very roots of one's being."* (Studies in the Theory of Emotional Development. New York. 1965.)

To be nobody but yourself in a world which is doing its best day and night to make you like everybody else means to fight the battle which any human being can fight and never stop fighting. ~e.e. cummings

In acceding to all the expectations of the Watchtower Society (expectations couched in terms that make it seem like they are the requirements of Almighty God, himself) the JW child can become a lifeless imitation - a clone - disconnected from any real sense of self. In a way, the true selves of JWs (especially children and teenagers) are gradually annihilated so that what remains can be exploited to the benefit of the Jehovah's Witness organization. A ghastly thought when you actually see it in print! Even worse when you feel it in action in your own life.

This means that if one ever chooses to leave the sect, one will have the daunting challenge of having to dismantle the false JW self, live with the fear and emptiness that entails, and work to find and re-acquaint themselves with their true self, long since buried under the false self. That was certainly the case for me. The Watchtower organization interfered with the natural development of my real self and my on-going connection to it.

*You wear a mask,
and your face grows to fit it.*
~George Orwell

*Tear off the mask.
Your face is glorious.*
~Rumi

While living in North York, I attended Glen Rush Public School. There was a large Jewish population in that area of North York, so much so that at least two thirds of every class I was in, for the four years I was there, was Jewish. This made it much easier for me to be a Jehovah's Witness in the school environment. Jews don't celebrate the Christian holidays (well ... most Jews don't ... a few celebrated *both* their Jewish holidays and the Christian ones), so there was less accent on Christmas and Easter in the art and music classes. I didn't feel like such an oddball and my Jewish school friends did not seem to consider me one either.

But our family was due for another move and soon we found ourselves further west in the city of Toronto, in an area called Islington. My father had found work in a garage owned by a friend and when we first arrived on Anglesey Street in Islington we had no idea that we would live in five different apartments on that one street. We made those five moves in seven years. We always had to move to a smaller apartment when my father did one of his disappearing acts. I recall a couple of times when the lease for our current apartment was almost up and Mom had still not found us a new place to live. She preferred to spend her time in the kingdom ministry rather than looking for a place for herself and her two girls to live. She always said *"Jehovah will provide"*. I was not so sure Jehovah had the time or inclination to find an apartment for us and worried that we would soon find ourselves on the street. Anxiety and worry were an integral part of my life growing up in a dysfunctional family *and* as one of Jehovah's Witnesses.

In Islington, as a young teen, I made a great non-JW friend named Enid Glover. Enid and I were together for grade 8 at Humber Valley Public School and then on into high school. Enid never seemed to mind that I was a member of a strange religion nor that I had to abstain from so many activities that were de rigueur for normal teenagers like herself. I now know that I experienced a degree of sweet relaxation when I was with Enid because I could be more real - more authentic - than I could be with my clone-like friends from the Kingdom Hall. They too had donned false selves and our rather vapid connections could only be from false self to false self. Hardly authentic, rarely enriching or even satisfactory. Times with my *"worldly"* friend provided moments when I was not subject to undue influence, pressure or stress and, therefore, did not have to prepare myself to "fight, flee or freeze" – moments when my nervous system and over-taxed adrenals could relax and just be.

In high school, Enid being one of the prettiest girls in the school, became one of the most popular too. She did not cast me aside as her popularity rose but tried to include me in as many of the extra-curricular activities that the Jehovah's Witnesses allowed. Our personalities meshed and we had some great, fun times together.

Once in some sort of naïve and foolish effort to intermingle my so-called 'worldly' friendship with Enid with the young, social crowd of Jehovah's Witnesses, I brought her along with me to a party of JWs in downtown Toronto. Can't imagine what it was in me that imagined I could merge these two disparate parts of my life. The gambit, of course, did not work. As my Witness friends talked with Enid and figured out she was not one of *"us"*, they shunned her there and then, and a pall fell over the whole gathering. Realizing I had brought a non-believer into their midst, I too was treated like persona-non-grata for having presumed I could introduce an outside, *'worldly'* element into the JW social scene. I learned my lesson, but my allegiance that night was to my friend and we quickly left that party together.

I was then, and am now, ever so grateful for Enid's friendship. We have remained in contact via letters and emails over the years. She was a better and more enduring friend than any Jehovah's Witness friends from my teenage years.

The requirement of the Watchtower organization for young people to isolate and exclude themselves from normal social interactions thwarts their natural development into competent, confident, socially-adept adults. No wonder so many former Jehovah's Witnesses have such a challenge re-integrating themselves into the world at large. It requires fortitude, determination and patience with oneself to negotiate the challenges as an adult that you should already have encountered, mastered and integrated as a child. Shame on the Watchtower Society for so cavalierly interfering in the normal stages of psychosocial development of JW children and teenagers. The good news is that as adults we can catch up and complete the developmental steps denied to us as young people in a controlling, exclusive cult.

Enid and I at Canadian National Exhibition in Toronto. Enid is on the left. We were both fifteen or sixteen at the time. We look like twins!

And you? When will you begin that long journey into yourself? ~Rumi

CHAPTER 15

Excluding Myself

During my time in high school most of the Canadian provinces were still loyal to the Queen of England. She was, in fact, also the Queen of Canada. That meant that every day of school opened with the class having to sing both national anthems "*God Save The Queen*" and "*O Canada*". In case you don't know, Jehovah's Witnesses give their allegiance only to Jehovah God's Theocratic Kingdom and to no earthly kingdom or government. That is why they don't fight in wars, do not vote, do not commemorate Remembrance Day each November 11th, and do not sing national anthems. We were instructed by the Watchtower not only to not sing any anthem but also to not even stand up in respect when the hymns were played in public places. While people of many different faiths and nationalities would stand in respect for any anthem, Jehovah's Witnesses had to remain seated for every anthem.

This rule of Jehovah's Witnesses along with many others, such as not celebrating Christmas, birthdays, Valentine's Day, Easter, Mother or Father's Day, Halloween, Thanksgiving, etc., make life very challenging for Witness school-age children, because so many school activities and projects are planned by the teachers around these celebrations.

My mother would sometimes come with me the first day of the school year in primary school to talk to the teacher and explain that I was not being disrespectful (huh?), but on religious grounds would not sing or stand for the anthems and could not with good conscience sing Christmas carols, make Christmas cards, participate in gift exchanges, celebrate birthdays, etc.

Most teachers tried to be sensitive and helpful in this regard -- probably because they felt sorry for the poor Witness child. However, in spite of the teachers doing their best to work around all the things prohibited a Witness child, the child was still in the school and still in the class while the other children were happily engaged in these activities. Not participating in these school projects and activities often makes Jehovah's Witness children the object of contempt, ridicule, bullying and/or ostracism by their classmates.

Being accepted by your peers is an important need for children. Children want to fit in and are looking for acceptance and affirmation by their cohorts. Jehovah's Witness children almost always stand out as different and a little bit odd to their peers. They can't do the things regular children look forward to and take for granted. It's hard for children to accept you when you are so markedly different. Always being different and always having to exclude myself from normal school activities made me anxious.

I remember feeling anxious and embarrassed at Christmas gift exchanges in the classroom, as it appeared that I was too cheap or selfish to give a gift. I truly felt more embarrassed about not being able to give gifts than I felt sad that I didn't receive gifts. I could not go around and explain my *"JW Christian position"* to each of twenty-five children, nor would they be interested in hearing it. So while the children exchanged Valentine cards every February, I sat alone at my desk having no cards to give. Many children would walk over and give me a Valentine's Day card anyway. Then I felt even worse because I did not have one for them. If you are or were a JW, you know exactly what I am talking about.

One year I secretly bought and made Valentine's Day cards to exchange with my classmates. I had so much fun selecting which card I would give to each student! But the act of giving them was marred by my realizing the teacher was watching me and knew I was going against my faith and my mother's expressed wishes. Oh the guilt I felt for participating in that 'evil' celebration! Such silly, harsh burdens imposed on JW children. Of course, the truth is that these requirements of the Watchtower Society served their perverse purpose of keeping us separate from worldly activities and, thereby, more under their influence.

Think about it. A Jehovah's Witness child has the desire to participate, to give, to belong and yet if they follow their natural impulse to participate with their peers, they are doomed to feel bad about themselves and to feel guilty before God for breaking the rules. Their little minds are saying an eager and innocent *"yes!"* to a particular experience. But if they follow their *"yes"* (inner desire and impulse) they will, in almost the same breath, if they have been brainwashed well enough, be told "*no!*" by their own conscience. They may even experience guilt for having the desire to participate in normal school activities. How crazy-making is that?!

A Jehovah's Witness child goes to school every day well aware that they may be surprised with an assignment or activity from which they know they must exclude themselves. I realize now that this was a mild form of everyday trauma for me. I continually experienced low-grade anxiety wondering what the next humiliating scenario would be, how I could anticipate it, minimize its impact, and then worrying how I would be viewed and treated by my peers afterward. As a young JW worry, anxiety and hyper-vigilance became constant companions.

An example of this would be an impromptu school assembly that gathered all the classes in the school in the auditorium to hear speeches, be entertained ... whatever. All assemblies in the auditorium in our schools began with everyone standing to sing "*God Save The Queen*" and the assembly closing with the singing of "*O Canada*". The Watchtower cannily framed refusing to participate in the singing of anthems as another opportunity to demonstrate our love for and obedience to Jehovah God and his Kingdom *and*, of course, to give a witness. The organization made Jehovah God an exceptionally hard task-master.

To avoid being the only student not standing and not singing at a school assembly, I slowly distanced myself from my friends and classmates in order to be at the tail end of the group on the way to the auditorium. That way I could arrive last. By so doing I hoped I could stand outside the auditorium door until after "*God Save The Queen*" was sung, and then slip into a seat unnoticed in the darkened auditorium ... that is if a teacher didn't intervene and order me get into the auditorium.

As the school assembly unfolded I was always alert to any signal that it was about to end. Somehow I had to anticipate the timing in order to get up and out of the auditorium before everyone was asked to stand and sing "*O Canada*". I could not bear the humiliation of sitting there while everyone else stood and sang, so I developed a habit of going to the bathroom near the end of every assembly - thereby missing the singing of the anthem and looking like a total jerk while remaining seated through it. This meant there was a lot of hypervigilance and worry – wondering when to leave and go to the washroom, and wondering how long to stay in the washroom so that my timing was just right. All Jehovah's Witness children undergo similar experiences of humiliation and diminution, as well as the *internally-anticipated* embarrassments. Unpredictable humiliations cannot but raise a young person's anxiety and lower their self-esteem, ultimately making them more pliable and obedient to the cult ... and a nervous wreck.

The result was that I was always anxious about being blindsided by something not allowed by JWs being the next activity scheduled by the teacher or school administration. Living like that is not only anxiety-inducing but also a form of chronic worry and chronic trauma for Jehovah's Witness school children. Unpredictable stressful events take a heavy toll on a child. Recent research into chronic unpredictable stress reveals that beyond having deleterious effects on body systems, it actually changes the structure and functioning of the brain. (Childhood Disrupted, 2015)

Those of you who are Jehovah's Witnesses or ex-Jehovah's Witnesses, are all too familiar with these anxiety-producing predicaments foisted upon JW children - not by the schools - but by the controlling group of men known as the Governing Body of the WBTS who set the rules for what Jehovah's Witnesses are allowed and not allowed to do. Most of them have never had children and have little sensitivity to the distress, turmoil and damaging effects created by their arbitrary rules - nor do they seem to care, as it serves their purposes as stated above.

Another challenging activity for any young JW is going in the door-to-door preaching work every weekend. The neighborhoods where we would preach were assigned to us by the elder presiding at the pre-service meeting. I dreaded being assigned to preach in a neighborhood where any of my schoolmates lived. As a teenager I could not imagine anything more horrifying than knocking at the door to give a Watchtower sermon and have the door opened by a friend or acquaintance from school. Pure humiliation!

Mom always tried to see if she could get us assigned to an area that was not in our neighbourhood. Most of the time she was sympathetic to my need to avoid possible ridicule and humiliation, and I was always grateful for that.

While accompanying my mother in the field ministry we met two well-known, Canadian journalists and television personalities. One of these was journalist and radio commentator Gordon Sinclair Sr. who literally screamed at us about the Watchtower's blood policy. It was so unnerving to be yelled at while in the service - even if they were right. Journalist and TV personality, Betty Kennedy always graciously accepted the literature my mother offered. Sinclair and Kennedy, were weekly panelists on the long-running, nationally broadcast television quiz show, *"Front Page Challenge"*. Not knowing who you would encounter or how you would be treated in the obligatory preaching work was another form of unpredictable stress that can take a toll on the health of any child.

While in grade ten, I was informed by my bookkeeping teacher Mr. Zobel (in the Business & Commerce program I had selected in order to be equipped to find part-time jobs while I pioneered), that at the graduation ceremony that year awards and scholarships would be handed out for all grade levels. I was not graduating, but I had received an award for my good grades. Mr. Zobel told me that all recipients of the awards would be seated on the stage so that handing them out could proceed quickly and the real ceremony of distribution of the diplomas to that year's graduates could begin. I said *"Okay"* meaning *"Okay, you've given me the information"* not *"Okay I'll be there"*.

That day I told my mother that I would not be going to school and would not miss out on any important work because of the graduation ceremonies. I did not want to be sitting and not singing the anthems while parked on the stage where everyone could see. She understood that I wanted to avoid the public humiliation did not insist that I go. Then the phone rang:

Me: *Hello*

Mr. Zobel: *Mr. Zobel here. Just calling to remind you about the award presentation today, Bonnie. I noticed you weren't in class this morning.*

Me: *Okay, thank you for the reminder.*

Mr. Zobel: *You are coming aren't you? I'm presenting your award.*

Me: *No, I'm sorry but I won't be there.*

Mr. Zobel: *And why not?*

Me: *Well ... if you recall, as a Jehovah's Witness I do not stand for or sing national anthems and I thought it might be embarrassing for the administration and for myself if I was on the stage, not standing or singing, through both anthems.*

Mr. Zobel: *(silence) ... You make your way here by 2:30. I will escort you onto the stage after the singing of "God Save The Queen" and off the stage before the singing of "O Canada". You must come and receive the award you have earned.*

Me: *(silence) ... Alright ... (sigh) ... I'll be there.*

I still really did not want to go to receive an award, but his offer to help me save face was so thoughtful I could not refuse. Mr. Zobel was good to his word and escorted me on and off the stage at the key moments so that I did not have to display my Jehovah's Witness disrespect and peculiarities in public. He found a way to spare an anxiety-ridden Jehovah's Witness girl from public humiliation (and much internal stress) and I made sure he knew how grateful I was for his kindness.

CHAPTER 16

The Principal's Office

At the time I started high school, a decision had to be made about what educational program to choose. There were not that many options back then, but considering my goal of pioneering I was fortunate (Witnesses are not allowed to say "*lucky*") - I was lucky - that there was that previously mentioned Business & Commerce option.

I dared not consider having any sort of interesting or lucrative career, for I was going to be a full-time pioneer or even a missionary for the cult. The skills I could learn in a Business & Commerce course seemed perfect for finding a part-time job as a typist or bookkeeper. The Watchtower Bible & Tract Society encourages its youth to aspire to be pioneers. The sect maintains tight control on its rank and file by keeping them busy with Kingdom ministry activities and in menial jobs to earn the bare income they need to survive.

The organization wants you to announce God's soon-to-be-established Kingdom, distribute their publications and lure more people into the JW fold - BUT - they do not want to pay you a cent for the sacrifice of your time, energy or future financial well-being in order to accomplish this for them. Back then we had to devote one hundred hours (you cannot include the hours you spend travelling to visit people in this one hundred hours - only the actual time you spend talking to people, so in fact you are giving them way more than one hundred hours of your time) every month and because you aren't paid by them you must squeeze a part-time job into your schedule as well – and be content to live like a pauper.

All that to say, there is then absolutely no need for a young Witness to think about furthering their education at university. We were told that there are so many bad influences in a university milieu that could pull us away from *"the truth"*. The governing body was (is) afraid that you might learn something that could liberate your mind - and - worst of all you might acquire some critical thinking skills that could help you break their spell of control. The Governing Body maintains control over their adherents by keeping them from gaining any sense of personal competency or power via an education, satisfying career, or the attainment of professional and financial success.

I accepted that higher education was not a dream I could entertain. It was just not an option for me. My future was planned by the Watchtower Society and keenly anticipated by my mother. If I wanted to please Jehovah, the elders, the congregation and my mother, there was only one choice for me - the full-time pioneering work. Somehow my ability to dream for myself, to plan for a personal future had been neutralized. I thought that by suppressing my curiosity and sacrificing my future I was pleasing Almighty God, Jehovah. So sad.

So to that end, I enrolled in the Business & Commerce program at Burnhamthorpe Collegiate Institute. After two years there, some of us were relocated by the school board to continue the next two years of the program at Etobicoke (pronounced "Etobico" - don't ask me why) Collegiate. Shortly after the move to the new school, all the newly arriving Business & Commerce students were given a long, general exam from the school board and we all promptly forgot about it.

Always being seen as a bit weird by most of my classmates because I was a Jehovah's Witness (no blood, no birthdays, no dancing, no smoking, no sports, no drugs, no rock concerts, no mini-skirts, no Christmas, no dating, etc., etc.,) it always felt good to get top marks in the class. There had to be something I could do!

So besides being considered a bit of a 'goody-two-shoes' because of all the religious rules I adhered to, I was also considered a bit of an egghead ... but, it seemed, a likeable enough one. I had worldly friends that I hung out with during the school day even if I could not hang out with them on evenings or weekends. I did not feel like a *total* outcast.

One day over the school's P.A. system, the school secretary said: *"Bonnie MacEwan to the principal's office. Bonnie MacEwan to the principal's office."*

The whole class looked at me and snickered. It was assumed that anyone called to the principal's office was in big trouble. I shrugged my shoulders, rolled my eyes and chuckled too. It did seem funny to hear 'Miss

Goody-Two-Shoes' summoned to the almighty principal's office. What could I possibly have done to be summoned there? Because of my JW-prude reputation, I actually enjoyed a moment of being viewed as being 'in trouble', and I walked out of the room to see the principal with a bit of a swagger that was intended to convey, *"See - I'm not such a goody-goody after all"*. I had to sit for a while in the waiting room outside Principal, Mr. Evanson's office. Has anyone ever been shown into a principal's office the moment they arrive? The nervous students are always given time to think about their possible offense. I could not imagine what I had done wrong, and I now had several minutes to mull it over. Maybe it was the things I could not do or refused to do because I was a Jehovah's Witness. Was the school now going to object to my opting out of so many of their routine activities? Would I have to try to explain and defend the religion and my JW list of what was permitted and what was not, again? What a drag.

Finally Mr. Evanson's secretary showed me into his office and pointed to the chair I should take. Mr. Evanson was reading papers spread out on his desk. I sat down nervously. I don't think I'd ever had a direct exchange with the principal before this.

Principal, Mr. Evanson: *We've received the results of the test all of you students took a couple of months back - the test from the school board. It seems you did very well.*
Me: *Oh ... good.*
Principal: *So well, in fact, that we really must advise you to change programs. You are definitely not in the right program. A Business & Commerce high school degree will not allow you to proceed on to university.*
Me: *Well that is not really a problem, because I have no intention of going to university.*
Principal: *Why on earth not?*
Me: *Well, it's not easy to explain, but as a Jehovah's Witness I will be devoting my life to ... a kind of ... missionary work after I finish school.*
Principal: *(silence while staring at me and frowning) ... Missionary work?*
Me: *Well, we don't really call ourselves missionaries. I would be what is called a pioneering publisher of the good news of God's kingdom for the Jehovah's Witness religion..* (I knew what I was saying must sound really *"woo-hoo"* to Mr. Evanson.)
Principal: *(clearing his throat) ... Look ... you could always do the ... missionary thing ... after university. You must think about your education and your future*

now. There will always be time to be a missionary later, if you still want to ... Think very seriously about this, young lady.
Me: There is no point. My family is not in a position to send me to university anyway.
Principal: That is not a problem. With the marks you seem to get we would have no problem finding you a scholarship - at a few different universities in fact. To that end, you need to switch into a Liberal Arts program immediately.
Me: Well ... it's all very flattering to hear, but I really don't feel that I should switch programs since I know I won't be attending university and I will need the business skills to support myself in the pionee... 'missionary work'.
Principal: (silence) ... Perhaps we need to have this discussion with your parents present.
Me: Only my mother could come and she totally supports my plans for the future.
Principal: Please don't dismiss the idea just yet. Give it some thought. I have spoken with Mrs. Young (a Literature teacher that I had a good relationship with) and she would like to have a chat with you too.
Me: Okay ... but really, sir ... I know I won't change my mind.

As I type that conversation now, it makes me sad. I know that there was a part of me that was secretly fascinated by the idea Mr. Evanson proposed. However due to thirteen or fourteen years of indoctrination, I could not allow myself to consider a future other than the one the Watchtower and my mother wanted for me. And ... how many thousands more, just like me, have sacrificed their education, their futures and their lives for the WBTS?

It took a long time, and it was a long circuitous route, but eventually I got the university education that Mr. Evanson encouraged me to get that day. Before I embarked upon any studies, however, I had to figure out that being a Jehovah's Witness was robbing me of my life and find the courage and the way to leave. Then I had to figure out who I was apart from the religion and what I wanted to do with my reclaimed life.

Wish I could have let Mr. Evanson know that I finally escaped from the *"missionary work"* and followed his sound advice ... even if it was much later than he had hoped for.

I know how fortunate I was to be able to go to university and get degrees as a 'mature' student. I had a husband who was able and happy to support me, on every level, in such endeavors. Jehovah's Witnesses who leave the cult have to make major adjustments once the Watchtower activities are not the central factor in their life. Once out it can be a shock to realize there are huge gaps in their education and experience. Most leave with no higher education, no great work experience, no detailed resumes and no worldly contacts to give them references or point them in the right direction. Many realize, due to their immediate family obligations, that it will be difficult to catch up to their 'worldly' contemporaries in terms of education, experience, interesting work or standard of living. It can often seem as if there were just too many missed opportunities to make up for. Former middle-aged Jehovah's Witnesses can find themselves trying to do what they should have been doing in their twenties, had they not been in servitude to a cult claiming to be a religion.

Even worse, because of Watchtower claims that the end of the world is just around the corner, besides not getting an education many ex-JWs did not attend to acquiring adequate insurance policies, health-care coverage or pension plans. Few ever gave any thought to creating funds for their children's college educations. Many took menial jobs so that they could devote most of their time in the required preaching work and gave up any thought of home ownership or other income-building investments. Once they reclaim their life and their right to freedom, outside of the Watchtower's influence, they have the daunting task of trying to catch up and provide for their future and the futures of their children. The Watchtower Society is guilty of unduly interfering with and adversely affecting so many lives. These adverse effects, unfortunately, can be experienced for years after getting out.

Let yourself be silently drawn by the strange pull of what you really love.
It will not lead you astray.
~Rumi

CHAPTER 17

Working Girls & JW Creeps

About a year and a half after our family moved to live in the west end of Toronto, my father took off again for some new adventure connected to a job in the far North. This time, I think, he worked as a large machinery mechanic for a mining company, but it's hard to keep track of all his travels and changes of employment especially when he was so far away from home. Things became tough for my mother when Dad suddenly stopped sending part of his paycheck to pay for the family's living expenses. Perhaps my parents had a disagreement and he decided if she did not like what he was doing, she should just find some work and support the family herself. But Mom always felt too insecure to test her competencies in the big, bad working world and preferred to confine herself to her JW door-to-door activities. She, like all Jehovah's Witnesses, had been very carefully programmed to be afraid of "*the world*" - one of the many phobias the organization instills in their followers.

So Mom told me that she had again applied for "*Mother's Allowance*" from the government. I learned many years later that there is no such thing as "*Mother's Allowance*". We were on welfare. She invented this name, it seems, to spare me from knowing how desperate our plight really was, and I imagine to preserve my dignity. My irresponsible, father, knowing my mother's frugality and resourcefulness, probably figured we would survive just fine on welfare, and my mother preferred not to have to work in Satan's world when she could work for Jehovah and receive money from the government while so doing. Yes, somehow conveying to government agencies that she was incapable of working and thereby qualifying for *"Mother's Allowance"*, enabled my mother to spend her days in the field ministry on behalf of The Watchtower. This dishonesty did not seem to bother my mother's so-called *"Bible-trained conscience"*. For her, it must have been like employing *"theocratic warfare"* – dishonesty in service of advancing Kingdom interests. Living on welfare required, however, that we move to a smaller one bedroom apartment down the street. My sister and mother shared the only bedroom and I slept on the couch in the living room. I had no bedroom, no proper bed, no closet and no privacy as a teenager during that time. Mom was a good homemaker and though we had no money for frivolous things, we ate well (she could make a delicious meal from the most meager ingredients) and were always well-clothed due to her sewing skills and generous gifts of used clothing from well-to-do sisters in the congregation.

Babysitting was a way that I was able to earn some spending money during those tough times. One couple who lived in the basement concierge apartment in our large apartment building frequently requested my babysitting services. The husband was a fireman and often worked long stretches where he was away from his family for 48 to 72 hours at a time. The wife worked part-time as the concierge of the building. Sometimes when her husband was on one of his long shifts, she would ask me to look after their two small children for an evening. When I arrived at their apartment the children would already be in bed and she would invariably still be getting dressed. She wore slinky party clothes with lots of dangling jewelry and tons of thick makeup, especially gooey red lipstick. She always said she was going out for *"a little night out on the town with the girls"*. I figured that must be what worldly people do and really didn't think much more about it.

This woman would then arrive back home after her *"night out with the girls"* around 4:00 a.m., a little tipsy, disheveled and giddy. Since I had been there, by this time, for about 8 hours and she paid me $2 per hour I would be owed $16. She would pay me the $16 and always gave me $5 extra as a tip! That would be like a babysitter receiving a $25 tip in today's dollars! I was too naive and inexperienced to figure out what was really going on, but looking back I am sure my mother knew exactly what this woman was doing. (I always regaled Mom with stories about how this woman looked as she left for her *"night out on the town with the girls"*, and how disheveled and 'out of it' she was when she returned.)

This suburban housewife was probably out 'working' a hotel bar, - for a little extra cash – or excitement. Obviously with the kind of tip she gave me (none of my other babysitting customers ever tipped me) she must have had a lot of clients and made a lot of cash on each of those evenings! The tip was probably a bribe to make sure I didn't speak about any of this with her husband. Guess she had not figured out that I was too naïve to have intuited what she did and that I was being paid a bribe to keep my mouth shut. I find it interesting that my mother never objected to my babysitting for an occasional 'working girl' who was cheating on her husband and engaging in both immoral and illegal activity. My JW Mom let her daughter work for a woman probably prostituting herself and let her accept payment from those working-girl, ill-gotten gains. The money allowed me to purchase clothes and school supplies. Mom's practicality and monetary needs would occasionally override the moral codes she espoused. And I, naïve, young JW that I was, remained completely clueless about the real source of my earnings until many years later.

Sometimes, however, my mother was naive too. When I was about fifteen Mom began to allow me to go to parties hosted by young Jehovah's Witnesses in their parents' basement recreation rooms. She had once heard a brother at a convention say something to the effect that *"our young people have to walk a very narrow road, so at least give them the entire road"*. She seized upon that comment from the platform to buttress her non-interfering, generally relaxed parenting style, and I did not object! I know as JW mothers go, I had a pretty good one.

The parents at these JW social gatherings were usually upstairs and there was music, dancing, food and non-alcoholic beverages. Sometimes young brothers from Bethel would show up at the party bringing their own supply of beer to drink covertly during the get-together. There was a sister, a few years older than me, that took me under her wing and drove me to and from these parties, but that did not last for long. As time went on, brothers (young, single brothers - some from the Toronto Bethel) would offer to drive me home from the parties. My mother assumed this was just fine because you could certainly trust Bethel or pioneer brothers who loved Jehovah to not engage in any inappropriate conduct. Ha! Bethel brothers were the worst. I knew my naive mother had really misplaced her confidence in those men living in the repressed, male-dominated environment of the Bethel. Mom let me go out at night with brothers who were much too old for me. She implicitly trusted that they were guided by Bible principles in everything they did because they were working at the Toronto Bethel, or as pioneers in Kingdom service. Some turned out to be far from trustworthy.

One pioneer brother in his twenties (eight or nine years my senior) and I engaged in what I thought was going to be just a bit of kissing as we were standing just inside our apartment door, after he drove me home from a Bible study. (Yes, we were out alone in field service together.) My mother and sister were not at home. Before I figured out what was happening, in the middle of the kissing, he tightened his grip on my wrist and forcibly shoved my hand down the front of his pants, instructing me to *"Hold it."* Hold his erect penis, that is. My first impulse was to obey the command of a male voice. (Horrifying to admit, but true. I had been trained to obey men and for a couple of excruciating seconds, I did.) I had no experience with the mysteries and miracles of male genitalia and was aghast that a penis could morph into something of that size and solidity. I wrenched my wrist away from his grasp and pulled away from him. Fortunately, he was smart enough not to persist and seeing my shock, he left. Instinctively, I used the double-bolt lock on the door. I was sixteen, inexperienced, alarmed, ashamed and confused. It did not even occur to me to think of the episode as being one of abuse of a minor, but I did have the feeling of being used. I was shaking, ran to wash my hands and face and then threw myself on my mother's bed sobbing. I felt disgusted, afraid and ashamed. What had I done?! It did not occur to me to condemn only the brother. I slid into self-condemnation and self-loathing. My mother and sister would soon be home so I had to find a way to get a grip on myself. The only option was to push all the feelings down. I did manage to pull myself together, told no one, and forced myself to carry on. While I struggled to act normally and go on with my life in spite of these feelings of worthlessness, that pioneer brother went on to become an elder in the Watchtower organization.

It's clear that I was a needy, teenage girl looking for fatherly affection and did not understand that I was seeking it in all the wrong places and in all the wrong ways. Looking back, I see that naive and vulnerable as I was, I was fortunate to not have had an encounter with some other JW creep who decided to exploit my vulnerability and neediness and force me into doing something I was not ready for. Clearly my mother was not the only one who was too trusting of, and too naïve about, some of the JW brothers.

A pioneer brother (a good friend of the former), hearing through the grapevine that I had a summer job in an office, telephoned me at work and invited me out for lunch. He, too, was quite a bit older than me, attractive, and I was surprised, flattered and a bit baffled by this invitation. I didn't think he knew I was alive. I was not the only sister who would jump at the opportunity to go out with the handsome yet elusive H.B. We agreed upon a restaurant near my place of work and planned to meet there. I was particularly nervous, really wanting to hit it off with him and perhaps be invited out again. A girlfriend from our Kingdom Hall couldn't believe I was actually invited out by *the* H.B. and I, too, couldn't believe my good fortune.

H.B. and I enjoyed a pleasant conversation over lunch, chatting about our lives, trivialities and mutual JW acquaintances. Then over a cup of coffee, H.B. unexpectedly pulled a couple of flashy watches out of his pants' pocket. (Better than a penis, right?) He launched into a sales pitch trying to convince me that I really needed to purchase one of these watches. Any onlooker would have thought he was trying to pawn stolen merchandise on an unsuspecting teenager. What a sleazy way to trap and pressure someone into buying something they did not seek out, want or need! I really should have been smart enough to figure out that there was an ulterior motive to this invitation to lunch.

I was embarrassed and deflated when I realized selling me a watch was the real motive for his invitation. Being fair-skinned the humiliation made me blush and I could feel my face turn beet red. I mumbled something about having no need for a watch and prepared to take my leave. The humiliation began to turn to anger, at him and myself. How could I have been so naïve as to think that the much-sought-after, JW heart-throb would have actually wanted to date me? Well, I may have been naïve, needy and gullible, but H.B. really blew it when he thought of me as an easy mark for his sleazy watch-selling enterprise. I may not have known how to manage my girlish fantasies, but I did know how to manage my limited supply of money.

I got up and left him with his watches and the lunch tab, and headed back to work ... humiliated and crying ... again. A kind, worldly woman in the office listened to my sob story and tried to comfort me. All my illusions about H.B.

(and myself as being worthy of his attentions) had been shattered. Was this how he supported himself as a pioneer - preying on vulnerable, young sisters in the truth to make money? Now that's sleazy.

Another experience was 'with' a Jehovah's Witness pioneer brother at a district assembly. He and I had paired off a few times - sometimes simply sitting beside each other and chatting at circuit assemblies or at gatherings of young Jehovah's Witnesses. One time that we paired off together was when a group of us went horseback riding and out for pizza after. Perhaps he developed some notion that after a few group outings and conversations at assemblies, we were boyfriend and girlfriend and that I somehow 'belonged' to him. He asked me out a couple of times after the group horseback riding outing and I refused due to other commitments (the best excuse I could find). I was not interested in pursuing a relationship with him.

Now this district convention was outside of both his and my assigned convention area, so he should have had no idea of my plans to go to it. Perhaps he just decided to attend it, too. While there, I had the sense of being stared at. When I turned around, there he was, standing scowling at me with his arms crossed over his chest. It was a cold, threatening pose and something told me to just pretend I had not noticed him. The first couple of times that I sensed and then spotted him staring, I thought it must just be a co-incidence. But then the sister I was with noticed it too and assessed the whole thing as downright creepy. He kept popping up wherever I went in and around the stadium, and his angry stare began to feel menacing. Being with a group of friends, I did not want to encourage his interest or attraction by waving him over ... besides he'd creeped me out too much by now. For two days he followed me at a distance and glowered at me from afar. It was very unsettling. Sometimes his presence made the hair on my arms stand up on end. As the stalking persisted throughout the duration of the weekend (in fact, I could never have named his behavior as 'stalking' back then), I did my best to not dwell on it. It really didn't enter my mind to confront him, because it never occurred to me that I could *really* be in any danger. After all he was a pioneer servant of Jehovah God and we were at a Watchtower convention! Now I know that I could have been at serious risk by someone who was so disturbed he felt the need to stalk. I met my future husband at that convention while being stalked by this well-regarded pioneer from my circuit back in Toronto.

Another time a brother in his early twenties moved to our congregation from a different city. After he had been in our congregation for a few weeks he button-holed me after a meeting and informed me that since he was new in the area and didn't yet know any of the young JW crowd, he thought it was my Christian duty to bring him to get-togethers and parties and introduce him around. His request (really it sounded more like an order) took me aback. I stammered something to the effect that I usually went to such events on dates (obviously the organization had not come up with any chaperoning requirement back then) and didn't think it would be appreciated if I brought along another brother. He insisted that it would be the kind and Christian thing to do. Not knowing what to say, I found a way to excuse myself and talk to someone else in the Hall. Upon arriving home I told my mother how this brother had tried to twist my arm to get me to bring him along to parties with me, and to my relief my mother affirmed that I had no obligation to help him manage his social life. She said that it had been inappropriate for him to ask me to do so, that he was a grown man and he did not need a teenage girl to be his social secretary. I felt for him, but not enough to drag him around with me on my dates!

Of course, there were many really nice brothers whose company I enjoyed too. But nice is never quite as interesting unfortunately, as strange, aggressive or inappropriate! I have highlighted the creepy incidents with JW brothers to demonstrate that being a Jehovah's Witness does not necessarily make someone act with Bible-based ethics and respect.

One brother I did care for seemed to be a less-involved Jehovah's Witness, one who engaged in activities in the world that other JWs were afraid to explore. He pursued a higher education by attending university and studying journalism. That was certainly out of the norm for young JWs! This brother was also a jazz drummer and would sneak underage me into a jazz club called "Giorgio's" in downtown Toronto to hear up-and-coming jazz groups. He was so much fun to be around and he was a real gentleman. He was educating himself and talked about things that were new and exciting to me. He treated me with respect. During one Christmas season, each time he picked me up for a date he would sing, *"Oh, by gosh, by golly, it's time for mistletoe and Bonnie."* I still think of him when I hear that song. Funny, how he appeared to be the least indoctrinated of the brothers I dated, yet was one of the most intriguing, fun and honorable.

These random recollections about my teenage experiences with some JW brothers, have pulled me away from the chronological order of this memoir. Let me return to my high-school days in my mid-teens.

One day, I arrived home from school to find my father sitting like a long-awaited, slightly uncomfortable guest, in the living room. My mother was in the kitchen making something special for him to eat and kept her back to me, thus allowing for my own, true response to this surprise.

Dad was back! I ran to him, hugged and hugged him, and sobbed uncontrollably on his shoulder. I had not seen him in a year and a half. It was *so* good to see him again. From what I could read in my mother's demeanor, he was back to stay and that made me *so* happy! We were a family again! My heart swelled with hope that we would finally enjoy the family togetherness, stability and normalcy I had been missing. Soon we moved to a larger apartment on Anglesey Street - to make room for Daddy.

CHAPTER 18

Conditional Acceptance

Soon after my father's return, it became apparent that Mom had imposed certain conditions on him if he wanted to rejoin the family. He had to study with an elder in the congregation and he had to attend Sunday meetings at the Kingdom Hall. I don't believe my mother had any expectations of him knocking on people's doors in the field ministry … yet. It's really impossible for me to imagine my introverted father consenting to go door-to-door. I can barely imagine him grudgingly agreeing to my mother's other JW-related conditions.

The presiding overseer of our congregation came to our apartment once a week to study with my Dad. This brother could not have been more unlike my father on every level. He was younger than my father, an ebullient extrovert and a successful businessman. My introvert father was none of those things and even as a teenager, I wondered how Dad could ever relate to this man. My mother, sister and I would leave the apartment to allow the JW remedial work to proceed uninterrupted. While I really liked this elder, I imagined him getting my father to read exhortations from the Watchtower or other publications that showed how Jehovah would want a good husband and father to behave in a family. No matter how diplomatic this elder tried to be, for my father it had to feel like he was being rapped on the knuckles for his failings. Hard for any man's ego to take. The visits of the elder always made me feel vaguely apprehensive.

I recall my father coming to a special Sunday talk and Watchtower study at the Kingdom Hall. A high-ranking elder from Toronto Bethel was scheduled to deliver the public talk. Having an orator from Bethel was always deemed a special occasion.

Ninety-nine per cent of the brothers wore suits to our Kingdom Hall meetings. My father did not own a suit. He had no need of one as he was a car mechanic and 'occasional adventurer'. Heads turned as he entered the Kingdom Hall wearing a sport shirt with no tie and not even a sport jacket. He had to see all the heads turn, stare, and make silent judgments. He had to sense the critical whispers wafting like a quiet breeze across the Hall. I felt so bad for him. Sitting among all these financially comfortable, white-collar, middle-class brothers at the Kingdom Hall, I could imagine my Dad comparing himself to them and coming up short. All of my father's now required interactions with the JW community gave me a sense of foreboding. How long would he be willing to endure these impositions that always seemed to end up as comparisons and humiliations?

That Sunday the special guest speaker from Toronto Bethel was Leo Greenlees - the same Leo Greenlees mentioned earlier who later served as a member of the Governing Body in Brooklyn, N.Y. He was a good-looking man with a beautiful smile, dancing eyes and a head of gorgeous, prematurely white hair. I always enjoyed his talks, perhaps because of his lilting Scottish brogue. With all the kerfuffle after the talk, as brothers and sisters crowded around Leo (Bethel brothers who are of the anointed class and who will reign in heaven beside Jesus Christ are special, you know) my father was no longer the center of attention because of his attire, or lack thereof - to the relief of my mother, sister and myself.

By the way, as a young JW in Toronto, I did not hear any of the rumors about Leo Greenlees engaging in a homosexual affair. If the rumors were true, such conduct is an example of the hypocrisy and double-standards occasionally at play among some members of the Watchtower leadership. I am not shocked by anyone's sexual preferences or sexual expression. I am disappointed by members of the leadership within the Watchtower organization who prohibit certain behaviours, while engaging in them secretly themselves. After the way most of us had been taught to think about the Governing Body and Bethel, it's a bit disconcerting to imagine prohibited activities actually going on within the walls of 'the sacred houses'! Recent lawsuits and news articles reveal that pedophiles have been able to act out and hide out inside congregations of Jehovah's Witnesses across the globe – some with the knowledge of the particular congregation's body of elders and even the Watchtower leadership itself. I count myself lucky to have had no experience with, or knowledge of, any of that.

Back to the rules and conditions both overt and covert in my little family. I know it was never my mother's intention, but requiring my father to study with an elder and requiring him to attend Sunday meetings all seemed to end up diminishing and demeaning him. How could that make him want to be a part of the Watchtower organization? How could having to submit to such humiliations endear him to my mother and family life? How could conditions that made him feel 'lesser than' make him feel able to reliably and happily step up and provide for his wife and children? They surely could only demoralize my psychologically fragile father even more. And they did.

Let's get away from all the clever humans who put words in our mouth.
Let's only say what our hearts desire.
~Rumi

CHAPTER 19

The Slap

I was about fifteen, preparing to go to out in service on a Saturday morning when I ran from my bedroom to look out the big living room window to gauge the weather - in order to determine what clothes I would wear. Back then women wore slips under their dresses and I didn't think it mattered if I went to the living room in my bra and panties covered by a slip. My body was more covered than it would have been in a bathing suit at a public beach. Perhaps the seemingly immodest impulse is evidence I was still not used to having a male (my father) in the house. (By the way, the living room picture window looked out upon long stretches of back yards from the well-to-do homes the next street over. The houses were hundreds of yards away so no one could have seen my scantily-clad body at the window.)

My father, seeing me run into the room, jumped up from his chair, and out of nowhere called me a *"brazen hussy"* and slapped me across the face. A *"brazen hussy"*? Whoa! The slap and slur shocked and shamed me. I was dumbstruck! I wasn't used to being called names and certainly was not used to being slapped by either parent. No one had told me of a new rule in the family about not peeking out the window while wearing a slip.

I now realize that my bourgeoning womanhood must have disturbed my father in some way or other, and he was probably trying to slap down some of his own "*brazen*", unexpected impulses. It was evident to me, even then, that he too was shocked by his violent reaction to my sudden half-dressed appearance in the living room.

Whatever was going on with him, I felt shamed and deeply hurt by the stinging slap and nasty reproach. Neither of us knew how to speak in that moment about what transpired. There were no words of apology from him to try and repair any emotional damage. We both just shut down in shock and dismay. There were obviously no sophisticated communication skills nor much emotional intelligence at work in our family.

A few days after the slap, I was standing at the bus stop across from our apartment building, on my way to school. As I stood there my father came out of our building and I realized he must be coming to catch the bus too. Darn! He didn't usually leave for work at this time, so I was surprised and felt really uncomfortable to see him walking over. We had not looked at each other, nor spoken a word to each other, since the slap. Would I now have to sit beside him and 'make nice' on the bus?!

Several other people were also waiting for the bus. Once my father arrived at the bus stop he stood at a distance from me, behind the other people, and I did not turn and acknowledge his presence. Surely, a good daughter would greet her father. But on that day, I did not. I knew I was breaking some unwritten family norm, but still staggered and stinging from the slap - in that moment I didn't care. My injured, hurt ego pulled rank over any daughterly love in my heart.

"You have to keep breaking your heart, until it opens." ~Rumi

When the bus finally arrived I boarded and purposely found a single seat where no one could sit beside me. After Dad boarded, he walked right past me to a seat near the back of the bus. He obviously sensed I was still upset about the slap and slur and that I did not want to be near him. The whole situation was so weird. After several blocks he exited the bus - out the rear door. Our eyes had not met, nor had we spoken. Anyone on that bus would have assumed we were perfect strangers. For all intents and purposes, at that moment, we were.

I was full of conflicting emotions. On the one hand I felt justified giving him the cold shoulder due to the insulting name he called me and, of course, the slap. On the other hand I felt guilty for ignoring my father in public - for acting as if he didn't exist. We had all been working hard to make him feel comfortable and welcome in the family with the hope that he would not take off on another 'adventure'. So while still seated on the bus, watching him disembark and walk down the street I was suddenly overcome with guilt and a profound sadness. I felt such sympathy for him - recognizing how hard his life must be. And now this poor, pressured, insecure man had a daughter who wouldn't give him the time of day. Back at home that evening neither of us seemed able to address the slap or what happened (or didn't happen) at the bus stop. In the time we had left as father and daughter, we never spoke of the slap or the bus stop incident.

Now, years later, as I recall the bus stop scene I am able to see a father who to the best of his sensibilities (which were severely wounded in childhood), perceiving the needs of his own emotionally-wounded daughter, picking up her signals to stay away, was perhaps trying to respect and honor her need for distance.

This story of the slap and the bus stop is a quintessential example of how damaged relational patterns are passed down as negative legacies from generation to generation. My father wounded me the way he had been wounded by his JW father – with repeated abandonments, which child that I was, perceived as rejections. Good student that I was, I replicated the pattern of rejection at the bus stop. Being members of the Jehovah's Witness cult offered no true help or healing for our ailing, dysfunctional family. The corporation-cum-religion's scope seemed to be too limited by its publishing/preaching imperative to be able to help a fragile, failing family.

Although my mother was deeply in love with my father, she had patterned her welcome back to him using the Watchtower organization's example of conditional love. He was welcome to return to his family on the condition that he toe the Watchtower line. Mom made the crucial mistake of thinking that the Watchtower Society taught and exemplified the ways of the one true God, Jehovah and that her family would be blessed if she could get us to follow in their ways. Instead of strengthening her union with her husband and the father of her children, this allegiance to the Watchtower organization. and her insistence that my father also obey its many rules, put the family's cohesion and stability in serious jeopardy.

Myself & little sister ready to go in field service, a few months after "the slap".

A wealth you cannot imagine flows through you.
Do not consider what strangers say.
Be secluded in your secret heart-house, that bowl of silence.
~Rumi

This being human is a guest house.
Every morning is a new arrival.
A joy, a depression, a meanness, some momentary awareness
comes as an unexpected visitor ...
Welcome and entertain them all.
Treat each guest honorably: The dark thought, the shame, the malice,
meet them at the door laughing, and invite them in.
Be grateful for whoever comes,
because each has been sent as a guide from beyond.
~Rumi

CHAPTER 20

One Rejection Too Many

One night, soon after the slap and the bus stop incidents, my mother, my little eight year old sister and I arrived home from the service meeting and ministry school around 10:00 p.m. to find that Dad was not there. That was unusual. Some suspicion stirred in my mother. She began to scurry around the apartment while my sister and I stood stricken at about the same spot in the living room where I had received the slap. Mom mumbled to us that a suitcase was missing … and so was Dad's shaving kit. She then began to search for a note. There was none. He had packed up a few essentials and snuck away while we were at the Kingdom Hall. I think this was one of the few times that he had not left information about where he was going and when he would be back. My mother, sister and I stared at each other with a chilled knowing. While we hoped he was gone off on another adventure, we somehow sensed that this time it was something more.

    I have no recollections of my specific thoughts or feelings at the moment of that discovery. I must have frozen with fear. I had to be horrified by the proximity in time between the slap/bus stop incidents and his departure. I had to have felt responsible on some level for driving my father away. I never told *anyone* about the slap, the reproach or how dreadfully I behaved at the bus stop … I felt too ashamed … too guilty. And now, it seemed, there was even more to feel responsible for and guilty about. It seemed like too much for a fifteen year old self to bear.

    Possibly in an attempt to bury any feelings of responsibility and not even thinking to hold my mother responsible, I privately blamed the

Watchtower organization for the disappearance of my father. As with most things there is rarely one cause or reason for any event. Family dramas are rarely either/or situations. Most emotion-laden situations are complex and multi-layered. Now, I know that there were many factors contributing to my father's disappearance - one of which was the demands my mother made of him with regard to the Jehovah's Witnesses. Another was the dysfunctional incidents with his oldest daughter. There may also have been private things between my mother and father that contributed to him leaving. All I know is that the Jehovah's Witness 'religion' had really brought a lot of hardship to my father's childhood and the imposition anew of this strict, judgmental entity in his life may well have been something he could no longer stomach. He knew how to disappear, and he did. We never saw or heard from him, or of him, again.

> *I have had worse partings,*
> *But none that so Gnaws at my mind still.*
> *Perhaps it is roughly*
> *Saying what God alone could perfectly show -*
> *How selfhood begins with a walking away,*
> *And love is proved in the letting go.*
> ~C. Day-Lewis,
> Walking Away

Soon after Dad's disappearance, Mom discovered "*Racing Forms*" hidden in a box and realized that he had been gambling - perhaps in a desperate effort to catch up to other family men he saw who had worked steadily for years and were now providing a comfortable life for themselves and their families. He had been betting on horses as some sort of desperate, get-rich-quick scheme. The scheme did not work, of course. Mom was soon informed that Dad owed a good chunk of money to racetrack bookies. My mother now had to try to find some way to pay them off. The bookies somehow knew about my father's valuable sets of "Snap-On" tools in their big, red metal boxes and suggested that my mother sell them to get them 'their' money. Mom did not want to sell Dad's beautifully organized sets of tools, hoping against hope the tools would be there for him to earn a living if or when he came back. Dad had again put my mother in a terrible position – now having to negotiate with sleazy underworld types to pay off gambling debts. Religious pressures, family misunderstandings, a deep lack of self-worth and racetrack debts must all have weighed heavily upon him, causing him to make many foolish choices. His default solution? Run away ... again. This time for good.

Even though all the above factors were at play in my father's departure, I know my young mind was probably convinced he left mainly because of how I had slighted and humiliated him that day at the bus stop. Down the road I had much psychological work to do to rid myself of the guilt (some of it justified and some not), and was finally able to forgive myself for being so insensitive to my Dad. I took the advice of Buddhist teacher, Steven Levine who says, *"... healing is: to touch or to enter with mercy and awareness those areas of ourselves from which we have withdrawn in anger or in judgment."*

I have forgiven my father for the slap, the nasty slur, and his many abandonments. I have forgiven myself for shutting him out and rejecting him in an act of childish retaliation. We were two wounded people who never figured out how to apologize to each other and make things right between us. Had we had more time, I like to imagine we might have found a way.

> "I must tell you that I should really like to think there's something wrong with me—Because, if there isn't, then there's something wrong with the world itself—and that's much more frightening! That would be terrible. So I'd rather believe there is something wrong with me that could be put right."
> T.S. Eliot
> The Cocktail Party

And so again Mom, Ann and I moved on the same street to a smaller apartment. My mother applied to renew her "*Mother's Allowance*", aka welfare, and busied herself in the preaching work. When she wasn't knocking on doors or preparing for meetings she would sometimes sit on her upholstered rocking chair consoling my little sister who sat folded in her lap, crying.

My father's disappearance was like a death in the family and all three of us were in mourning – whether we knew it, acknowledged it, or not. That image of my mother and sister sitting rocking, with tears rolling down their cheeks, is burned in my memory. I wondered then, if my mother would have the strength to go on without my Dad. I realized later, that against everything experience should have taught her, my mother never gave up hope that he would return.

After several years with no word of or from my father, my mother learned that she could have him declared legally dead and then been free, apparently even in the eyes of the Watchtower organization, to move on with her personal life. (If she remarried and somehow my father reappeared she would have been considered guilty of adultery, however.) There were a couple of brothers who made gestures of interest toward her, but she never gave up hope that Dad would return. So she did not have him declared legally dead. She continued to wait on him ... and, of course, Jehovah.

Around the time that we were still actively grieving my Dad's disappearance, a Jehovah's Witness family from England emigrated to our area and attended a congregation adjacent to ours. The handsome, blonde son of this family and I were attracted to each other and began to talk to each other almost every day by telephone. We went to a few JW parties together and sat together at circuit assemblies or special JW meetings. I really enjoyed his sense of humor and the attention he paid me, was quite infatuated with him, and he demonstrated a similar infatuation.

It wasn't long until a second JW family emigrated from England and moved into his congregation. This family had an attractive, raven-haired, buxom daughter a little older than me who immediately captivated his attention. Those two families, being from England, had much in common but I was convinced that those big bosoms weighed heavily in the diversion of his attentions. He came over one evening to see me. I hoped this meant he could see past her imposing assets and had chosen me to be his girlfriend. Not. He sheepishly disclosed he would now be exclusively dating the English sister.

I fell apart. I'd only known him a few months but I felt like my heart had been ripped out of my chest. I could not eat. I could not sleep. This went on for days. (It should be noted here that although I had felt stunned, sad, afraid and guilty after my father's departure, I had not, like my mother and sister, allowed myself to cry.) I was now inconsolable about the loss of this brother's affections and could see through my swollen, tear-filled eyes that my mother was worried. She allowed me to miss school, meetings and service – encouraging me to rest and regain my equilibrium. In spite of these accommodations I could not seem to pull myself together. The grief-stricken crying went on for days. It felt like I was shattered.

When the reaction to an event is more intense than what the event really warrants, it is a sure indication that the reaction represents more than just the particular event. Clearly I was not just crying about the breakup with the English brother, although I was convinced that I was. When he told me he had placed his affections elsewhere and was leaving our relationship, I must have finally felt the full force of the pain and impact of my father's rejection and abandonment.

Of course, pain was not the only emotion ravaging my psyche. On an unconscious level I must have felt that I had wounded my father so deeply that he had no other option but to leave, so I felt crushed by his disappearance and even more by the guilt I could not speak. Mom did her best to help me with the feelings she was aware of, but no words, no consolation, no affection, no explanations or rationalizations could relieve me of my unconscious burden of guilt and the resulting despair. I was dealing with profound guilt, sadness and now the double wrench of rejection.

It is interesting to me, that during this period of a sort of emotional collapse due to stress from a myriad of adverse conditions, there was nothing from the scriptures or from the Watchtower literature that helped me. It seems the WBTS has little to offer that will help heal the wounds of immediate loss, the wounds of familial pain and the pain of conscious and unconscious emotion when you feel you may have inflicted pain on others. The Jehovah's Witness organization demands so much of its adherents and seems to have little to give in return during times of personal crisis. (I am speaking of the Watchtower organization, not the generally kind and supportive rank and file.)

Between all the chronic stress and anxiety I experienced as a JW child, the unstable family environment, the teenage hormones, the guilt, shame, abandonments, rejection and loneliness experienced during those years, I marvel that I was able to keep going ... but humans are resilient and somehow I did.

My mother was very loving and understanding during that time. She did not pressure me when I said I did not feel like going to the meetings or in service. I've always appreciated that temporary period of exemption and reprieve from the normal JW demands. All my reserves of energy were depleted and

Mom respected the evidence she saw that I needed to rest and recover. I know I was fortunate to have such an understanding JW mother. My mind took note that physical and emotional injuries produced exemptions from weighty JW demands, and as any trapped victim will do, I tucked that information away for future use.

I know you're tired, but come. This is the way.
~Rumi

CHAPTER 21

Ambitions

Life continues in spite of our pain or circumstances and sooner or later, the pain, angst and guilt heal, **or** get pushed down, and you begin to feel more engaged with life. That seemed to be true for my mother, my sister and myself - especially the part about the emotions being pushed down or buried. Buried where? In the furthest reaches of the mind and in the body, in the very cells of the body. Henry Wordsworth said, *"There is no grief like the grief that does not speak."*

What we do not realize is that when we push down or suppress our pain, we are at the same time cutting off our ability to experience other positive emotions like contentment, happiness and joy. We cannot cut off one type of emotion without inhibiting all emotion.

The suppressed pain sits there, waiting to be acknowledged. It waits for however long it takes for us to pay attention to it. It will resonate and quake with other pain that comes along in life, though we will not quite understand why we feel so bad about seemingly simple, albeit difficult, events. The suppressed pain seems to accumulate into 'one clump', and when we are able to feel some of it, we will feel the weight of it all and wonder why our expression of emotion seems so out of proportion. The pain buried in our body/mind, desperate to attract our attention, may even 'act out' by causing dis-comfort or dis-ease.

Mom kept busy with the Witnesses, as did we two girls - as much as was expected of us at our respective ages. My sister was busy with her little set of friends and I with mine (we are seven and a half years apart). We did our best to operate as a 'normal' single-parent family.

By this time I had acquired some skills at typing, shorthand and bookkeeping in that Business & Commerce program in high school - enough skills to get summer jobs with companies in downtown Toronto with Ontario Hydro, National Life Insurance Company and later on Lawyer, Frank Mott-Trille.

While working at Ontario Hydro I was assigned a job where I floated between departments filling in wherever help was needed, usually as a typist or stenographer. One week I was asked to step in as the subject of an industrial film being made by Ontario Hydro in conjunction with the Polaroid Corporation. The film was about the first use of Polaroid camera equipment to make "instantaneous" (their word back then) full color I.D. cards in a large company setting in North America. It was a full day of filming, with a director and other Ontario Hydro employees assigned to play roles, and was certainly more exciting for us than our usual office jobs. It was a glimpse of a professional opportunity, but since my future was already laid out for me by the Watchtower Society, I did not feel free to explore it.

Footfalls echo in the memory, down the passage we did not take, towards the door we never opened, into the rose garden. ~T.S. Eliot, Four Quartets

It's like watching Paris from an express caboose heading in the opposite direction--every second the city gets smaller and smaller, only you feel it's really you getting smaller and smaller and lonelier and lonelier, rushing away from all those lights and excitement at about a million miles an hour. ~Sylvia Plath, The Bell Jar

I have heard the mermaids singing, each to each.
I do not think that they will sing to me.
~T.S. Eliot

IDENTIFICATION CARD PROGRAMME

On August 17th, at Head Office, the Security Division initiated a new identification card programme, employing newly designed equipment capable of mass-producing instantaneous identification cards in full colour.

These ID cards were issued to regular employees who had temporary cards or none at all.

Below are some photographs taken of a subject going through the procedure of getting her new identification card.

In this photo, Miss Bonnie MacEwan is receiving her data card from Miss Terry LaPointe. She is required to sign the card and obtain a number which will be used to microfilm the ID card after it is completed.

Here is Mrs. Marlene Somers focusing the camera on Miss Bonnie MacEwan. After the photo is taken, it will be laminated, cut, microfilmed and sealed in a plastic wallet.

An Ontario Hydro Newsletter with snapshots taken during the filming process and the final color Polaroid ID card. Notice the 'high-tech' Polaroid camera!

One summer I was able to offer a few weeks of volunteer service as a typist to the Watchtower Convention Headquarters in Toronto. The big district conventions of Jehovah's Witnesses could not happen but for all the work of the pre-convention volunteers. One of the brothers in charge of the activities at the convention headquarters where I was volunteering had everyone intrigued and whispering. He was a young pioneer, in his early twenties and, more interestingly, had declared himself to be one of the anointed class. Whoa! It was rare to encounter anyone who was a member of the 144,000 anointed and in their mere twenties!

All of we young sisters in the typing pool were on high alert when this brother walked into the offices. There was a titillating curiosity that helped attenuate the boredom of our jobs. Could he really be anointed? How long had he known he was a member of the 144,000? What did it feel like to be young and believe you would reign beside Christ in heaven? How, actually did he know he was anointed? And, most importantly ... did he date? If so, who? (Rumors spoke of someone called "*Linda*" who showed up occasionally as a volunteer.) What would it be like to marry a member of the anointed if you weren't one? There was no possibility of ever sitting across from him during a break and having a chance to ask our nosey, impertinent questions. His body language clearly conveyed how busy, unavailable and disinterested he was in spending any break time with us.

This young brother was not friendly, helpful or supportive to those of us banging away on typewriters. Perhaps he was just preoccupied with his responsibilities, but to my curious eye he came off as rather arrogant and self-important. Perhaps he was insecure and unsure of his management abilities. Whatever the case, to those of us doing the grunt work at the headquarters, this young member of the 144,000 anointed appeared unusually closed off. If and when he smiled it was only the muscles of his mouth that moved. His eyes and the other muscles in his face did not move, and that was rather disconcerting. These peculiarities were so remarkable that I described his behaviors and demeanor to my mother each day when I returned home from convention headquarters. I recall describing him with the frequent use of the word "*creepy*". Mind you, I was about sixteen at the time.

When brothers with positions of authority, like JW lawyer Glen How or elders from Toronto Bethel made an appearance at the convention headquarters, this young brother put on a big smile, vigorously shook their hands, patted their backs, and became unabashedly solicitous and unusually sociable in their presence. It was clear to all of us in the typing pool that this brother had big ambitions and was attentive to those who, in the future, might be useful to help him attain his goals.

It was not often, as I circulated through all the events and activities of the Watchtower Corporation over the ensuing years, that I came across someone I immediately disliked and distrusted as I did this brother. Oh, did I forget to mention his name? David Splane. Yes, the same David Splane who is currently a member of the Governing Body at the world headquarters of Jehovah's Witnesses. Seems that his ambitions and behaviors paid off. (I've read that his wife's name is "*Linda*".) David Splane achieved his early, lofty goals, yet during his tenure at the top of the pyramid, he has thwarted the dreams and ambitions of millions of rank and file members in this controlling cult.

David Splane

Funny, as I've watched recent videos of David Splane on YouTube or on JW broadcasting, it seems my teenage assessment of him was not far off. He still seems stiff, uncomfortable and formal - with a feint air of superiority. One has to wonder if being 'anointed' and a member of the highest level of the JW corporate pyramid (especially during recent years with so much damning internet exposure) has turned out to be all he hoped it would. One expert on dreams and ambitions, Marilyn Monroe said, "*Dreaming about being an actress, is more exciting than being one.*" I'll take her word for it.

CHAPTER 22

Collateral Damage

I was in my second last year of high school still facing the challenges that any Jehovah's Witness has in the environment of a worldly institution. It perplexed me how so many people in the world lived such seemingly happy, carefree lives when they didn't know Jehovah or the truth. Perhaps it was because they didn't have to worry about:

- the imminent arrival of the Battle of Armageddon when God would destroy all those who had not subjected themselves to his kingdom
- the imposed responsibility to warn, in the door-to-door preaching work, as many people as they could about this looming destruction
- remaining obedient and chaste so that they wouldn't be among the millions that would be destroyed
- Jehovah reading their thoughts and knowing everything about their inevitable thought-lapses into impurity and disloyalty
- being brought up before a committee of elders if in a moment of weakness they actually *did* something forbidden by the religion
- being rejected by all family members and friends if they ever decided to leave their religion

Though this tightly-controlled life as a Jehovah's Witness teenager was a bizarre way to have to live, I did my level best to co-operate with what the expectation-laden, threat-laden, fear-laden cult demanded of me. But there was a part of me that longed for just a pocket of carefree time. How I longed to be lighthearted and unburdened by unreasonable expectations from an outside authority! The burdens of being a Jehovah's Witness weighed heavily on my teenage self and were causing stealth damage to my emotional and physical health.

While most of the time I did my best to love Jehovah, serve Jehovah and be a good example of a Witness for anyone around me, I also developed a habit of quietly looking for ways to get out of going from door-to-door and to the meetings. My mother was still worried about my fragility since my father left and since the romantic breakup, and she continued to encourage me to *"rest and take it easy"*. I sometimes exploited her concerns for my well-being by trying to find legitimate health reasons to stay home from Witness activities, thereby following her suggestion to *"take it easy"*. I did not want to lie, so I would scan my body for any hint of an ailment or physical malaise. If I searched long enough I could almost always find something (an ache, a pain, some fatigue) that I could use (without too much guilt) as an excuse to stay home from a meeting or field service. Mind you, with all the anxiety and worry I experienced due to my family circumstances and the unreasonable expectations of being a Jehovah's Witness, I know my adrenal glands must have been spewing out a lot of adrenalin and cortisol to cope with the real and the anticipated psychological emergencies inherent in being a Witness child. Persistent high levels of adrenaline and cortisol can have adverse effects on the body's systems, so not all of my physical issues were fabricated. But, for the Watchtower any discomfort or suffering experienced by their followers was a non-issue – just incidental, unavoidable collateral damage.

My mother was particularly vulnerable to any signs of illness in her children as she was always afraid of not having the money or means to call a doctor, or pay for hospitalization and/or medications. This made her bend over backwards to do whatever she could to keep us in good health even if it meant exempting us from meetings or field service.

For my part, my body was holding so much emotional pain and suppressing so many feelings and psychological issues that it began to exhibit actual pain and discomfort - probably as a signal to me. Now I know the signals were probably trying to say: *"Hey girl! You are not happy in the field service! Hey girl! How are you going to sit through another long meeting hearing the same old stuff?" "Hey girl, are you going to spend your life never doing a single thing you really want to do?"* Unfortunately, I received the physical signals that my body produced but I was unable to interpret their actual meaning. In fact I had no idea I could even look at aches, pains and illness as metaphors for psychological states. I just knew that I was experiencing physical discomfort. Because I wanted to avoid meetings and service I almost welcomed physical problems as they gave me a legitimate excuse to do just that. *"The worst curse to befall anyone is stagnation, a banal existence, the quiet desperation that comes out of a need for conformity."* ~Deepak Chopra

    I recall one Sunday afternoon, during a public talk when I felt so stifled, so uncomfortable that I thought I might physically explode. I kept shifting on the wooden chair, crossing and uncrossing my legs, massaging my neck - but to no avail. Finally I told my mother I could not sit there one moment longer and had to get out of the Kingdom Hall. To my surprise she did not frown, object, question or criticize. But home was three miles away. Mom arranged for someone to look after my little sister and to drive her home after the meeting. She then said she would walk home with me. My mother willingly left a meeting for me! I was so grateful to her for understanding, accompanying and not chastising me. She somehow understood I just had to get out of there.

    There was a palpable relief once out of the Kingdom Hall. The long, brisk walk home with my mother helped work off some of the tension. Too bad that I was unable to see the glaring message in that situation of acute discomfort. Actually, I was unable to get the message that I really needed to explode out of the cult, because the consequences of acting on my discomfort and dissatisfaction would be too drastic – too devastating. There seemed to be no option but to continue in the oppressive, yet mother-approved JW routine. My body was trying to help by screaming out my psychological needs with physical symptoms, but my teenage self was too indoctrinated and too unsophisticated to understand them.

You were born with wings, why prefer to crawl through life?
~Rumi

My high school graduation photograph.

Being raised in a fundamentalist sect limits an indoctrinated mind's ability to discern and understand metaphor. Fundamentalists such as Jehovah's Witnesses are taught a literal, verbatim interpretation of the *"divinely-inspired"* Word of God. They believe, that unless a scripture is clearly represented as allegory or metaphor it is to be interpreted literally. There is no depth and no sophistication in their thinking. In fact, much of their thinking is of a rather primitive nature. I did not learn how to extrapolate beyond what was revealed. I had been trained by years of sitting in Jehovah's Witness programming sessions (aka meetings) to take things as they were presented, to not think critically about what was said, to not be curious or ask questions about what was presented, or even about what life and my body were presenting to me. Religious programming had dulled and diminished my ability to discern metaphor, inference and layers of meaning.

There is, of course, no encouragement by Jehovah's Witness leadership to look beyond the obvious or to even imagine that there can be levels of meaning in a passage of the Bible, or in life itself. In fact the leaders have already filtered and interpreted the holy words for their followers who are actually encouraged to *"avoid independent thought"* (e.g. Watchtower Magazine, 01/15/83, p. 22). Thus, having accepted to submit their thinking process to a higher authority, rank and file members will experience difficulty seeing metaphor, nuance, inference, intimation, layers, depth and symbolism in their own readings of the sacred texts. How then, will they ever recognize symbolism or metaphor in their own life experience, behaviors or symptoms? And, how then, will they ever truly be or know themselves?

> *For I have known them all already, known them all --*
> *Have known the evenings, mornings, afternoons,*
> *I have measured out my life with coffee spoons.*
> ~T.S. Eliot

Although sometimes using physical ailments as an excuse to get out of JW obligations began as an immature teenage ploy, it gradually morphed into an unconscious psychosomatic pattern. Whenever I found myself in a situation where I was expected to do something I really did not want to do, I would often automatically develop some physical ailment. It was like my unconscious was trying to spare me from the psychological discomfort of indoctrination and proselytization by creating physical discomfort. How very accommodating, or so it seemed. My body was trying to give me legitimate reasons to not have to measure out my life in miserable, doled-out-doses of meeting after miserable meeting. Feeling physical discomfort or dis-ease gave me permission to exempt myself from the obligations and expectations being a Witness imposed. I'm sure this pattern of physical dis-ease to express repressed pain or inner conflict was not unique to me within the ranks of Jehovah's Witnesses.

If you were a JW back in the seventies and eighties you must have noticed how wives of circuit overseers invariably had many physical problems. Well, now you know why. Those women sacrificed any semblance of a normal life with a home and family. They sacrificed having any control over their own lives. As a result many of them were in an enormous amount of psychological conflict and distress which often translated into their bodies screaming in protest and even chronic illness.

This phenomenon is called somatization. It is a tendency to experience psychological distress in the form of physical symptoms. There is a chapter in my book "*Exiting the JW Cult: A Healing Handbook*" that highlights an amazing mind/body technique developed by John Sarno, M.D. for dealing with chronic pain or illness of psychosomatic origins. However, recent research demonstrates that the illnesses that beset so many Jehovah's Witnesses may have an even more sinister genesis and resulting impact.

In the book "*Childhood Disrupted: How Your Biography Becomes Your Biology, and How You Can Heal*", science writer Donna Jackson Nakazawa shares the study results of several research scientists including Seth Pollak, PhD, professor of psychology and director of the Child Emotion Laboratory at the University of Wisconsin. Jackson Nakazawa says "*...fifty children with a history of adversity and trauma showed changes in a gene that helps to manage stress by signaling the cortisol response to quiet down so that the body can return to a calm state after a stressor. But because this gene was* damaged, the body couldn't rein in its heightened stress response. Says Pollak, "A crucial set of breaks are off." This is only one of hundreds of genes that are altered when a child faces adversity. When the HPA (hypothalamus-pituitary-adrenal) stress axis is overloaded in childhood or the teenage years, it leads to long-lasting side effects – not just because of the impact stress has on us at that time in our lives, but also because early chronic stress biologically reprograms how we will react to stressful events for our entire lives."

Jackson Nakazawa further states, "… kids whose brains have undergone epigenetic changes because of early adversity have an inflammation-promoting drip of fight-or-flight hormones turned on high every day – and there is no off switch. When the HPA stress system is turned on and revved to go all the time, we are always caught in that first half of the stress cycle. We unwittingly marinate in those inflammatory chemicals for decades, which sets the stage for symptoms to be at full throttle years down the road – in the form of irritable bowel syndrome, autoimmune disease, fibromyalgia, chronic fatigue, fibroid tumors, ulcers, heart disease, migraines, asthma, and cancer."

Well … that explains a lot for those of us raised as Jehovah's Witnesses and subjected to the constant stress of chronic, unpredictable situations, deprivations, abuses and humiliations, doesn't it? As the title of Jackson Nakazawa's book states, our biography as a JW child can become our biology. Imagine the amount of both emotional and physical suffering the Watchtower Society has caused with its unreasonable expectations, undue influence, indoctrination, enforced social isolation and ever-present interference in the lives of families and children! But again, for the Watchtower, all the physical and emotional damage inflicted on those trying to conform to their arbitrary controls is mere collateral damage.

My story, detailing Watchtower abuses and the physical challenges that resulted in my life, is but one among millions. I encourage you to read Donna Jackson Nakazawa's books, "*Childhood Disrupted*" and "*The Last Best Cure*" to better understand how being a member of the JW cult may have adversely affected your on-going state of health, and the very manageable steps research scientists say you can take to reverse such effects.

In order to hide my true feelings about being a Jehovah's Witness I also had to summon up some acting skills. Most people had no idea how unhappy I was being a Witness. I studied the Watchtower, I gave comments, I gave talks, I knocked on so many doors, I conducted Bible studies with other teenagers in the congregation who were supposedly spiritually weak. I was used in demonstrations at circuit assemblies. I accompanied the circuit overseers (Eugene Rossam for one) and a district overseer (Joe Scaglione) in service and took them with me to some of my return visits. They seemed to think I was an exemplary young publisher. Why sometimes I almost fooled myself! The congregation used me as an example for other young Witnesses.

Years later, when no longer a JW, I joined an improvisational drama group called *"Women's Transformative Theatre"*. I remember the leader of the theatre group (a former actress and director from the U.S.) saying that I was *"a natural actress"*. Go figure. I just smiled to myself, thinking of all the years of experience I had acting - simply to survive as a Jehovah's Witness.

CHAPTER 23

Love & Marriage

In the summer that I was seventeen, working, and having a bit of extra spending money, a friend and I decided to go to a Jehovah's Witness District Convention, on our own. She had just been given a fabulous new sporty car (a Chrysler Barracuda) by her non-JW father and it was a sweet taste of freedom to take off, just the two of us, for a nice long drive to the convention city, stay overnight in a motel, perhaps see new cool guys at the convention, and … sit and listen to a few Bible talks when we weren't exploring other options!

It was at this JW convention that I met my future husband. We married two years later. He is seven years older than me and was already a special pioneer and the presiding elder of a French congregation in Quebec, Canada when we met. His mother was a devotee of the Jehovah's Witness sect (her whole family were active members, too), while his father was not a JW nor an adherent to any other faith. My love-interest's family had moved to Montreal when he was in his middle teens. He learned French in school and became fluently bilingual when he was assigned as a special pioneer to a remote town in Quebec. He went there as a twenty-four year old presiding overseer. Terry's parents and his two much younger brothers moved back to Waterloo, Ontario after Terry left home.

Terry and I eventually married in the Kingdom Hall at Toronto Bethel. (Mom had said that if I didn't marry him, she would!) Because I had no father in my life and my mother existed on her *"Mother's Allowance"*, Terry's family was kind enough to step in and finance the wedding. Young and naïve as I was, it did not occur to me that this meant I would have very little say in how our wedding and reception would unfold. For example, I particularly admired one brother, Bill Amos, who was beloved in the Toronto area and, who had babysat me as a toddler when his wife and my mother would go out in service. I would have liked for Bill Amos to be the one to give the wedding talk. Bill was a sensitive, loving man and a warm, gifted speaker. However, Terry's Uncle Art was a prominent Witness in the city of Toronto and was, in fact, what was then called the *"city servant"*. Terry's mother wanted her brother, Art, to marry us. I figured it was not an unreasonable request and went along with it. Truth was, I was afraid to object. Once I realized Bill Amos would not be giving the wedding talk, I asked him to take the photographs on our wedding day. As a well-equipped amateur photographer, he was happy to assume the task.

With Terry's Uncle Art being the one to marry us, the venue was changed from our little, local Kingdom Hall on Burnhamthorpe Road to the more impressive Kingdom Hall at the Toronto Bethel. Okay, I thought, Bethel is close by. That will not be a major problem. I was allowed to decide who would walk me down the aisle and chose my father's JW brother, Clifford MacEwan.

Terry and I were invited to meet with his Uncle Art to discuss the wedding ceremony. I assumed we had also been invited for a little "welcome to the family" supper so that Terry's uncle could get to know me in order to make the wedding talk a little more personal. How naïve of me. Terry's uncle dismissed his wife from the room after a brief welcoming chat. There was no 'welcome to the family' supper. Art proceeded to issue several non-negotiable instructions about how our wedding would proceed. As he talked, he directed most of his rigid instructions to me, rather than to both Terry and I. What could Terry's mother have said to him about me?

My dress and the bridesmaids' dresses were to be simple and modest. (Of course the dresses would be modest.) My Uncle Cliff and I were to walk with a normal gait down the aisle. No slow walking. (I had no intention of parading down the aisle in a typical, *"worldly"* wedding march.) Further, as I walked down the aisle toward the Kingdom Hall stage and my husband-to-be, Terry was not to turn around to look at me. That, Terry's uncle announced, would be akin to *"creature worship"*. He would not preside over anything that resembled *"creature worship"*. I had not heard of such a rule for any of my JW friends' weddings. In fact, I always took my eyes off of any bride walking down an aisle to sneak a peek at the groom, looking at and awaiting his beloved. Uncle Art seemed to be able to justify his covert misogynist attitudes with his Biblical beliefs and his JW organizational authority. He had determined that Terry looking at me walking down the aisle would be an act of *"creature worship"* and that was that.

There were other regulations enunciated by Terry's rule-obsessed Uncle, but I had heard enough and just tuned-out. I don't think I had ever felt so bossed around and intimidated by any elder than that evening as we were preparing for our wedding. There was no sense of being welcomed into the family. Art seemed to assume I would do something to turn the wedding ceremony into an event to glorify myself. Terry's uncle clearly enjoyed his Bible-based dominion over women and, it seemed, his misogyny would played out with me at our wedding. Ugh.

Terry's mother (Uncle Art's sister), Eloise, decided that since they were paying for the reception it would take place in the city where she and Terry's father lived - sixty miles away from where the wedding ceremony would take place at Toronto Bethel. All of our wedding guests would be required to drive sixty miles to the reception after the wedding! Neither Terry nor I had been consulted about this and I did not feel as if I could object. As well, Terry's mother never gave my mother the courtesy of including her in the planning of the wedding reception and my mother, already embarrassed that she could not financially contribute to her daughter's wedding, did not feel she could insert herself, uninvited, into the preparations.

Permit me a little digression here to help you understand the tense relationship between myself and Terry's mother. We had a rocky relationship from the very start. The first time I met her was when Terry brought me to his parent's home for a weekend visit. Terry and I had been seeing each other exclusively for a few months by this time. After the initial introductions, Terry carried our luggage up to the bedrooms. Once Terry was out of earshot, with a raised eyebrow his mother said: "So ... **you** came too." Shocked, I replied, *"Terry didn't tell you he was bringing me with him?"* She shook her head to indicate "No", perhaps imagining that by not uttering the word aloud she was then not lying. When I went up to unpack my suitcase (in the room of one of her other sons who had kindly vacated his space for me) it was clear that accommodations had been made for a female, overnight guest. Terry told me that he had, of course, informed her he was bringing me. She, a supposedly good Jehovah's Witness, had lied to make me feel unwelcome, and it worked.

Later that evening, after a family supper, I was washing the dishes as Eloise dried them and put them away. She insensitively talked about Terry's infatuation with some pretty pioneer sister in Montreal, claiming that they were *"just so great together"*. True or not, (it was not) it was an unkind thing for her to say. She then dipped her hand into the sudsy water in the sink where I was washing her dishes and mumbled something about the water not being hot enough. She turned on the hot water tap to heat up the dishwater. It was scalding! I told her it was becoming too hot to bear, but she kept her hand on the faucet and allowed more and more scalding-hot water to pour in. As an eighteen-year-old, I did not have the tough, weathered hands of a longtime homemaker. My hands turned an angry beet red. Was it just my imagination, or were her actions abusive?

That evening as Terry and I stayed up later than the rest of his family, his mother arose from her bed to admonish her adult, pioneer, elder son that it was late and he should go to bed. How disrespectful of, and embarrassing for, her adult son. He ignored her. The next morning, about 8:00 a.m. while getting dressed I heard her crying in the hallway outside the bedrooms. Through her sobs, she was telling Terry it was impossible for her to function if he and I were not going to keep to their morning schedule. (I think she had expected us to go out with her in Saturday morning field service.) That was it! I had had enough. I packed my bag, found Terry and told him that I wanted to leave as it was more than clear I was not welcome in his mother's home. Terry's mother, in spite of being a respected, devoted Jehovah's Witness, was neurotic, mean and duplicitous. Her other two daughters-in-law have their own strange stories to tell. Fortunately, Terry and his two brothers are anything but mean – unlike what I experienced with their JW mother and JW uncle.

Back to the wedding: The congregation I frequented was a tight one with lots of extra-curricular congregation activities and parties. While for most of those parties I was not of an age where I could drink liquor, I still noticed that these parties were well-supplied with wine and beer. I never saw anyone get drunk at these get-togethers, but I did notice that, the brothers especially, enjoyed access to alcoholic beverages.

Terry's mother had another brother (not Art) who had become weak spiritually, began to drink, and became an alcoholic. He had been reproved by his congregation, to his JW family's horror. Terry's mother arbitrarily made the decision that since Terry's now sober uncle would be at our wedding reception, there would be no alcohol served – not even a pay-for-your-own-drinks bar. She was adamant that she would not have our wedding reception be responsible for setting the now sober uncle on a path to drinking again. While I empathized with her concern for her brother, it occurred to me that we may as well call this celebration a 'wedding assembly' with all the rules and interdictions that were being arbitrarily imposed.

(Unfortunately, a few years later this alcoholic uncle died while on a drunken binge. He had returned to his home while drunk, collapsed and died on his own porch. It was my understanding that his JW family would not respond to his knocks on the door – but don't quote me on that. The JW funeral was a travesty, in my opinion. The brother who gave the talk made it clear that Terry's uncle would most probably not be resurrected in *"the new system of things"*. It was such a disrespectful funeral service, concentrating on what Terry's uncle had done which went against the JW religion and finding little of merit to say about the man as a human, a son, a husband, a father, a brother, an uncle, a friend. If I had to make a list of moments as a JW that indicated to me this might not be the true religion, Terry's uncle's funeral was one of them.)

I will spare you all the details of our wedding and reception, most of which was lovely, but I will share a couple of moments that were far from joyful due to the attitudes and regulations laid down by Terry's Uncle Art. The unwelcome regulations stemmed from who he was as a mean-spirited person, strict JW, and from what personal, controlling behaviors he believed he could impose by being a high-ranking Witness in the city.

On the wedding day, my Uncle Cliff picked me up at our home and drove me to Toronto Bethel. Bill Amos, who had been at our apartment taking photographs of the bridal party, followed close behind. Once at Bethel, Bill Amos had a plan of where he wanted to take more photographs. Uncle Cliff and I followed his instructions about where to stand. Bill took several photos on the steps leading up to the entrance of Bethel.

Once inside Bethel, there were more stairs to climb as the Kingdom Hall was then on the second floor. Bill wanted more photographs on those stairs and while Uncle Cliff and I posed for those shots, Terry's Uncle Art burst through the doors from the Kingdom Hall, clenching his jaw, barely controlling his anger and said I should stop being self-centered having photographs taken while all the guests sat waiting in their seats. He instructed me to stop all this *"vanity stuff"* and get myself into the Kingdom Hall immediately. We were dumbfounded. I was on the verge of tears - but said nothing. Who would talk to a nervous, young bride about to walk down the aisle like that? I felt so demeaned and was embarrassed that Bill and Cliff had to witness such a nasty scene. Bill Amos and my Uncle Cliff were also taken aback and both encouraged me not to worry about Art's untimely and uncalled for outburst, and to do my best to enjoy the marriage ceremony. That was going to be hard. I just wanted to sit down right there on the steps and bawl.

Literally shaken from being berated like a naughty child, I took my Uncle Cliff's arm and we made our way, *quickly* down the aisle to the tune of *"Praise God with Me"* from the JW songbook of the period. Uncle Cliff's son John played the song on the Kingdom Hall's piano (My cousin John MacEwan, I have recently been told, is now head of the Legal Department in the Watchtower's Canadian headquarters). For a brief moment, Terry followed his Uncle's stern orders and stood gazing at the wall behind the stage with his back to me. He then defied his uncle's rule and turned around, met my gaze and smiled. His smile gave me the courage to proceed in spite of my distress. I had had to use all the mental and emotional strength I could muster to put the abrupt, unwarranted scolding out of my mind, so that I could concentrate on my husband-to-be and our marriage vows.

By the way, the day before the wedding I developed a mysterious case of laryngitis. No sound came out when I tried to speak. This made speaking my marriage vows (or responding to Uncle Art's nasty tirade) difficult and interesting. I sounded like a man with a husky whisper. Perhaps my ever-accommodating, prescient body was telling me that at nineteen years of age I was much too young and immature for marriage vows and was trying to make it impossible for me to speak them.

It was a very 'dry' wedding reception and I recall while on the dance floor hearing brothers say to each other, *"Wouldn't a Dow go good now?"* ("Dow" is a brand of beer owned by Molson Breweries in Canada and that phrase was one of their advertising slogans.)

All the JW beliefs-driven interference, impositions and bizarre personal ideas about how our wedding should proceed put a damper on our special day, but, thankfully, not enough to have any long-term effect on our relationship. Our marriage has been a long and successful one in spite of its strange debut orchestrated by our strict, misguided, and unduly controlling JW relatives.

With our immediate families in front of the WBTS text for that year "Here I am. Send Me." From left to right: Terry's Father, Terry's Mother, my Mother, me, Terry, my Sister

Standing outside Canadian Bethel after our Jehovah's Witness wedding.

Once married, I was bumped up from being a regular pioneer to a special pioneer and Terry was given a new assignment as presiding overseer in a larger French congregation in Sherbrooke, Quebec.

I could write a long essay on the conditions of our first home in the dark, dank basement of the old Kingdom Hall edifice in Sherbrooke. Most of the walls were covered only in tar paper and the place reeked of mold. We shared the gloomy, claustrophobic basement with five other pioneering women – three of them nice, one a little quirky, and one just plain ignorant and with a degree of personal hygiene that would impolite to describe here. Suffice it to say we had to regularly insist that she bathe and then insist she go back to the bathroom and clean it after she bathed.

It was a shock to my nineteen year old self to be thrust into such a raw, uncouth environment. We even had a mentally-challenged brother who attacked the outside wall of our basement residence with an axe! Although I loved my husband, I just wanted to get out of that dark, dank, almost windowless basement and go 'home'. I really missed natural light and, of course, I desperately missed my mother and sister. The degree to which I missed my mother obviously correlates with my level of readiness for marriage at the age of nineteen, and how unprepared I was for any sort of communal living with heretofore strangers. The truth is, I was too young for both marriage and special pioneering in a province where I could not understand or speak the language. It was tough. Fortunately, we did not stay in that dank, dismal basement for long. Yes, I had been raised by a mother often on welfare, but the living conditions provided for JW pioneers in that city were like living in a third world hovel. While subsisting on welfare with my Mom, I lived like a spoiled princess in comparison. I was completely unprepared for such conditions, while Terry was able to view it as just another adventure. Thank goodness he was able to talk me through it all.

In a few months we moved to a little bungalow on a hill in a rural farming community, just outside of Sherbrooke. The only way we could afford to live there was if we shared the house with another couple. The brother was an elder and pioneer, while his wife worked full-time as a schoolboard secretary. We all became good friends and had many great times together while living in that little house on the hill.

Why should I stay at the bottom of a well, when a strong rope is in my hand?
~Rumi

CHAPTER 24

Special Pioneering

We settled into our life in the little four-room bungalow. What a relief to get out of the horrid Kingdom Hall basement! Our farmer landlord and other folks along that country road must have looked at the two couples living in the little house on the hill suspiciously, wondering what two couples were doing living together in the same house and probably imagining the worst. We plowed ahead with our responsibilities as special pioneers, and Terry with his added responsibilities as presiding overseer of a congregation of approximately one hundred people.

I recall returning to our little home on the hill late one night after going out to study the Bible with an interested couple in a town thirty miles away. We drove through freezing rain and sleet to get to this Bible study. The drive back to our little house on the hill was harrowing. Cars were spinning out on the highways and ending up in the ditch. We were sure we would end up in the ditch too. Once we turned off the highway and our house on the hill was in view in the distance, our car could just not negotiate its way up the road coated in glistening layers of ice. Terry tried and tried to coax the car up that hill, but the tires could not get any traction.

There was a full moon that night and its light was reflected by all the ice. Though there were no street lights, the winding road up to the house was visible. We waited a while and then tried again to urge the car up the hill, but to no avail. Our only option was to leave the car at the side of the road and do our best to get up the hill to our home on foot. Sheet lightening lit up the sky now and then and the thunder seemed to both menace and mock us.

Neither of us could get a firm footing while trying to walk (slide) on the sheer ice. After a couple of falls where we could have split our heads open, or cracked our teeth, we did the only thing left to do. We crawled up the long, winding hill on our hands and knees - dragging our book bags beside us. I crawled in front while Terry pulled up the rear sometimes walking, sometimes crawling, hoping to catch me if I started to slip backwards. With only panty hose on my legs (sisters could not wear pants to meetings or in service, even in winter in those days!) by the time we finally got to the house my knees were scraped and bleeding. The memory of us crawling, probably the length of two football fields, up to our house on the hill boggles my mind. Just another little adventure while dutifully serving Jehovah!

The couple that shared our house had their own difficulties that night. When their car seemed on the brink of sliding off the road into the ditch, the sister impulsively jumped out of the passenger seat, trying to brace the car from its slide. She just missed being pinned under the car, as gravity took over on the ice and the car slid into the brink. We've had a lot shaking heads, and a lot of laughs about that absurd night. It was surreal at the time.

We had many frightening, weird, and even creepy experiences participating in the full-time field ministry for the Watchtower Society as well as working in menial jobs to supplement the $50-a-month stipend we each received from the WBTS. Let me share a few of them here:

In our first months special pioneering I just accompanied Terry or other pioneers and publishers in the kingdom ministry. I could not understand a word of what was being said. I recall often asking, after we left a home, what the householder had been so angry about. Whoever I was with would reply that the householder was not angry at all. What on earth was I talking about? I soon figured out that many French Canadians in that area had a way of yelling loudly when they talked and I kept interpreting their style of talking as anger. It took a while to get used to that.

Once while sitting at a householder's kitchen table, while Terry conducted a Bible study with an interested woman, I just tuned out because I could not concentrate on every word of something I could not understand for a full hour. It was near the end of the Bible study and my eyes began to wander – looking around the kitchen. Suddenly my eyes fell upon a birdcage holding a completely featherless, skinny, excruciatingly ugly bird. It was a ghastly sight and before I knew what happened I let out a blood-curdling scream that frightened the woman and shocked Terry. A lot of back and forth translation went on as Terry explained to the woman that I had been horrified to see a bird in that condition and as the woman explained the bird had some revolting illness. Poor Terry – the last thing he expected was for his young wife to shriek out in the middle of a Bible study!

We conducted a Bible study with a woman in an isolated house on a lonely country road. Her husband was in jail, so she had a large half Doberman, half German shepherd dog (more the size of a small horse) that sat on her porch guarding herself and her children. We wondered if this dog was there to protect her from some mafia-type adversaries of her husband. We had no idea, but she had warned that the beast was vicious and to approach with caution. Each time we went there I expected the lunging, barking creature to break its chain, attack and clamp its huge jaws and pointed fangs around one of our throats. We always held our book bags up around our heads to protect ourselves as we walked by. Somehow we survived and lived to tell the tale.

I went every couple of weeks on a back-call on an older English-speaking woman who lived alone with a few, much smaller dogs. Once, while sitting on her filthy couch sharing some Bible verse, one of the dogs jumped up to sit beside me. The dog then proceeded to pass gas for about five minutes and the odor was foul. The woman could hear what was happening and enjoyed watching me squirm. She had a smirk on her face, as I sat there with my Bible and literature on my lap, having to breathe in the foul odors of her farting animal. As I left and walked down her gravel driveway, I recall thinking to myself: *"Why am I wasting my life doing this?"*, *"How is this work benefiting anyone?"*, *"What is the matter with me that I continue to do this?!"* I was disgusted with the situation and myself for submitting to it.

Terry was once making a return call on a woman and no one answered his knock. He knew the woman had several small children and could hear them making noise inside. He knocked again. No answer. Finally a little boy opened the door and my husband asked if he could speak to his mother. The little boy looked at him with gigantic eyes, saying nothing. Terry, becoming concerned that these little children had been left alone, asked if his mother had gone out. The little boy shook his head to indicate *"no"* and pointed to the closed door of a coat closet. Yes, the woman was hiding from my husband, the annoying Jehovah's Witness, in her closet.

Terry drove school buses in the early morning and then again in the afternoon to supplement the $100 a month ($50 each) we received from the organization as special pioneers. (He had a few harrowing experiences driving those buses on the hilly highways and byways during the harsh winters of Quebec.) Since we were living in a French milieu and I did not yet speak French I did not immediately find any part-time office work. I did some housekeeping and babysitting work to earn a few dollars here and there. I had a one-day-a-week mother's helper job for a couple of English university professors. Their little two year old girl, would walk up to me and say, all in one breath, "*SHIT! ... I'll behave*", over and over again. I found it amusing and did nothing to try and curb her need to test my limits. I guess it had shocked previous employees and she wanted to see how it would work on me. The large dog in that home was another matter. As I took care of light housekeeping duties while looking after the children, I quickly became aware that every time I crouched to clean a low shelf, or crouched to wipe up a spill on the floor, the dog would lunge at me with its fangs bared. And so, to avoid being attacked I had to learn to tidy up, clean and deal with the children without ever crouching or letting the dog see me do it. Not easy. All this nonsense to earn a little money as a domestic while simultaneously a slave of the Watchtower.

So we spent our days in the door-to-door ministry, and on the side tried to earn a little money to survive – often ending up in some sort of crazy situation -- all due to being special pioneers for the Watchtower Society. It seems so absurd now and such a monumental waste of our young married lives. Due to our indoctrinated choice to special pioneer for the Watchtower organization, our first years of marriage were rather difficult … for me. On many levels I was deeply unhappy. The ways that this unhappiness manifested must have hurt, perplexed and disheartened my hard-working, loving husband. Our young-married days could have been, and should have been, so much more happy and carefree. Being special pioneers for the Watchtower stole much from us as newlyweds, though we probably would never have admitted it at the time.

Why do you stay in prison, when the door is so wide open?
~Rumi

CHAPTER 25

Undue Influence & Acting Out

Since hundreds of pioneering brothers and sisters who didn't speak French were coming from all over Canada to "*serve where the need was great*" in the province of Quebec, the Toronto Bethel arranged for a six-week French-immersion course which was to take place in a Kingdom Hall in the city of Montreal. I was invited to attend the course. This meant I would be separated from Terry for six weeks as he had to continue with all his congregation and work responsibilities in Sherbrooke.

Once in Montreal, I was assigned to share a donated studio (one room) apartment with a circuit overseer's wife, for the duration of the course. I had known her slightly before I was married in Toronto. She was an attractive, slender woman of Scandinavian descent, about eight to ten years my senior. She had married a circuit overseer much older than she, after the death of his first wife. We had to share the double bed of a pull-out couch during the six weeks.

This roommate was a sweet person, but having been in the circuit work for a few years by then, she was used to receiving special treatment and having her every need and whim met by deferential congregation members. She had, I was soon to discover, a real sense of entitlement. In fact, we had been assigned our very own little apartment for the duration of the course precisely because of her status and special entitlements as a circuit overseer's wife. She was probably not too thrilled to have to share it with another of the students.

It seemed that she liked how I styled my long hair and announced that I should do her hair in a similar style each morning, with the expectation that I would be thrilled at the opportunity. I replied that how she styled her hair seemed just fine and suggested we should each look after our own grooming needs in the rush to get ready every morning. When she realized I might not accede to her wishes, as she was accustomed, she became angry, lectured me about what the kind, Christian thing to do would be ... and then ... turned on the tears. She clearly felt entitled to have me work fixing her hair every morning for those six weeks. I felt I had no choice but to acquiesce to her undue influence, and so every morning of those six weeks I begrudgingly styled her long blonde hair.

It did not feel good attending to her hairstyling needs because every night I had a terrible time sleeping and was exhausted and miserable each morning. Why? Because this delicate, fair-haired waif snored like a four hundred pound truck driver. Many times in the middle of the night, during those six weeks together, I dragged a blanket and pillow to the bathroom to try and fashion a bed in the bathtub. I hoped to create a space where I could finally get some sleep. Needless to say in the mornings I felt more like wringing her neck than creating ringlets for her requisite chignon!

We sat side by side in that Watchtower French course, two blondes with a similar hairstyle - clones in many more ways than one. Seems so funny now. It was not amusing then.

Terry & I at a party celebrating the completion of the Watchtower sponsored French course.

When that French course was over I certainly had a better understanding of the language, but was still a long way from being comfortably fluent in the language. At a circuit assembly not long after, a district overseer (initials S.S.) informed me that it would be good for all the brothers to see an example of what the Watchtower Society's French-Immersion Course had accomplished. I told him I did not feel ready to speak French in front of a large audience. He said it would just be a very brief interview. "*I'll ask you "this", and then "this", and then "this". All you have to do is answer those three questions*", he said. "*You can surely do that.*" Terry stood there with his eyes urging me to accept this 'privilege'. I felt pushed into a corner, unduly influenced – trapped. Knowing a good, special pioneer should not refuse the request of a district overseer, against my own better judgment, I agreed.

This district overseer (later a member of the Toronto Bethel) was a fine brother, and a great public speaker. Why he barely used notes when he spoke from the platform. S.S. always seemed to speak extemporaneously and easily captivated his audiences! I arrived beside him for the on-stage interview. He thought he was asking the questions with the same words he had said he would, but he diverted from the promised 'script' I thought we had agreed upon, and asked me "*that*", and then "*that*" questions. He never asked me one "*this*" question. He interviewed me using compound sentences that I hadn't heard him speak when we discussed the interview.

My face went beet red. I didn't quite understand the nuances of each of his questions, but I did my best to compose some sort of response. I heard strange, unknown syllables come out of my mouth that sounded like unadulterated gobbledygook! I wanted to dig a hole and die. When S.S. realized he had misjudged my competence in French he hurriedly thanked me and brought the interview to a close by asking the audience "*Isn't she doing great?*" What else could they do? They all applauded as he gestured for me to remove myself from the platform.

The applause did not help alleviate the humiliation. I had disappointed and embarrassed this district overseer, my husband watching in the audience and myself. The circuit assembly audience must have felt uncomfortable and embarrassed for me as well. This could really qualify as an incident of undue influence. What better way to demolish someone's self-esteem! This all could have been avoided if, as an adult, I had recognized that I had the right to say "*No*" to the district overseer's arm-twisting. That brother had been trained to exert undue influence and unfortunately I had been trained to acquiesce.

The result was that we were both publicly humiliated. I ran down the halls of the school where we were having the assembly trying to find a private place where I could cry out my shame. *"What am I doing here?"* was the familiar question screaming in my mind. It would still take a while before the question became *"How do I get out of here?"*

A photograph at the circuit assembly where I felt unduly influenced to be interviewed on stage in French.

Slowly I began to master the French language and began to speak more fluently at the doors, conduct Bible studies, and give talks in the Ministry School. I did not have the ear for languages that Terry had, and never became quite as proficient in the language as he.

The French-speaking inhabitants of Quebec were very patient with the hundreds (probably thousands) of English pioneers, like myself, who were banging on their doors, trying to show them in ghastly, broken French how they needed to leave the Catholic Church and become Jehovah's Witnesses. I always felt embarrassed imposing myself on them with my English-accented, memorized French sermons.

Terry, because he had a non-believing father who wanted him to have an education, had studied art and graphic design at the renowned, Ecole de Beaux Arts in Montreal. A couple of his professors were part of the famous Canadian Group of Seven artists. He had studied art history, learned to sketch and paint, mastered the skills of a graphic artist and some photography and print reproduction skills, among many others. Since our marriage he had not really been able to use any of this university training. He was too busy with field service, responsibilities in the congregation and had no choice but to work at menial jobs (such as driving school buses) to supplement our income and meet our expenses.

One day, on a whim, Terry pulled into the parking lot of a printing company, went in and asked if they needed a part-time graphic designer. He talked with the owner for a while which gave the owner an opportunity to size him up. This man said he didn't need a graphic artist, he needed a salesman and he thought Terry would be perfect for the job. Once Terry felt confident that the owner of the printing company understood he would only work part-time, he accepted. Terry came back to the car elated. *"I just got a job as a part-time salesman! I'll earn a percentage on what I sell, but listen to this: He's giving me a weekly draw of one hundred dollars. We're 'rich'!"*

It sounds absurd to call $100 a week *"rich"* now, but back then it was over the top. For two poor special pioneers of the Watchtower Bible & Tract Society it felt more like a $1000 a week. We didn't tell anyone *"in the truth"* about the salary - they would have said we had become materialistic and were now at risk of becoming spiritually weak. (Apparently pioneers are now required to belong to a *"Religious Order of Jehovah's Witnesses"* and are obliged to sign a vow of poverty renouncing any right to work part-time to supplement the nominal pittance received from the Watchtower Society!)

Terry certainly owed years of public speaking practice and years of learning how to 'sell' the Bible message and Watchtower publications for some of the sales talents the new employer spotted in him. He did inherit a great deal of natural salesmanship abilities from his father, but it was as a Jehovah's Witness that he had honed his speaking skills, learned when to make the final pitch, learned how to overcome objections, etc. He was a great salesman and a few years down the road would become a successful businessman/entrepreneur. But he would be the first to admit that some of his managerial skills, leadership style and salesmanship came in some measure from his work as an elder, pioneer and convention organizer for the WBTS.

Now that we had more than a subsistence income, we decided to get our own apartment - the first one in our married life. It would also be the first time we had not, as a couple, been living communally. It was a brand new apartment and we were finally able to pull shower gifts and wedding gifts out of their boxes and set up a real little home of our own.

Of course we gave all credit to Jehovah, but in truth it was my husband who had done all the work to improve our impoverished Watchtower special pioneer lifestyle. Soon I, too, found a part-time job as a bookkeeper and was able to contribute to our subsistence income.

That year the city of Sherbrooke was selected to host a summer district convention. A circuit overseer was put in charge of all pre-convention preparations and came to stay for six weeks in Sherbrooke with his wife. Our Kingdom Hall was transformed into convention headquarters during the day. Terry and I were asked to work full-time in this office to set up everything necessary in preparation for the convention.

I enjoyed doing this office work much more than going door-to-door every day. We had a great personal and working relationship with the circuit overseer and his wife. We entertained them in our new apartment enjoying many evenings drinking home-made wine, talking and laughing around our kitchen table. This circuit overseer's wife was an example of what I had seen over and over again – forgotten women suffering from many nagging physical ailments that just never seemed to subside. Even then, I wondered if it was due to the required sacrifices of home, children, normality that they had made or been unduly influenced to make.

This circuit overseer had a great sense of humor and kept our work life at the Kingdom Hall light-hearted and fun. I began to notice that this attractive C.O. would often take me aside to share private observations or jokes. Sometimes he would hold my arm and whisper a funny or provocative remark in my ear. Now and then he would hold his hand on my back while he explained a task that he wanted me to take care of for him. Once, in a moment of levity, he pulled me really close and began to dance me around the circumference of the Kingdom Hall. (That now makes me think of the remark of George Bernard Shaw, "*Dancing is a perpendicular expression of a horizontal desire.*")

Now and then his eyes held mine for a beat too long. He was good looking, sensitive and charismatic and, had I not been in love with my husband, I can see how this whole scenario could perhaps have developed into something more. In the humdrum life of being a special pioneer spending our lives doing little that mattered or that held any interest, I have to admit I enjoyed this circuit overseer's flirtations ... and I've no doubt that at times I encouraged them and flirted back.

On the one hand I was flattered by his attentions. On the other hand, a part of me was troubled that a circuit overseer would behave in a way that could invite immoral (according to the Watchtower) behavior. Perhaps the repression of so many normal human instincts, as demanded by the organization, eventually forces a sort of acting out, even among the supposedly most spiritually mature - simply to relieve the pressure of so much suppression.

I recall another circuit overseer and his wife who were well-loved in Quebec. Both of them were extremely intelligent, charming, and wickedly funny. The circuit overseer shot out one-liners like a professional stand-up comic. When circuit overseers visited the congregations, rank and file members signed up to have the circuit overseer and his wife (sometimes accompanied by the congregation overseer and his wife) come to their home for a meal. The brothers and sisters went to a great deal of work and expense in order to entertain these representatives of the Watchtower Society.

One French Canadian couple in our congregation invited the four of us for supper during the circuit overseer's visit. The husband was a garbage man in a neighbouring community and his tiny, older, yet child-like wife cared for their home. They were on the periphery of the congregation because they were shy, uneducated, slow, and a tad unkempt. The wife always had greasy hands and a grey pallor to her skin. This invitation would have been a very 'big deal' for them. We, on the other hand, were all a little wary about eating a meal at their home – wondering if their kitchen was as unkempt as this sister seemed. In the car on the way there, the circuit overseer, knowing I was young and new to being entertained this way, was teasing me about what kind of food we might be served at the garbage man's home. Those remarks, while disrespectful, seemed benign enough as they were uttered only among the four of us in the car. I was nineteen and figured that this was how circuit overseers behaved in private in order to release a bit of the pressure of their regimented lives.

Once in their home for the evening meal, the garbage man and his wife did not join the four of us at their table. Instead they worked preparing and serving the four of us the meal. It demonstrated, to me, the high regard they had for the position of the circuit overseer. It also occurred to me that perhaps they did not consider themselves worthy to sit with them. I empathized, for on some level, I too, did not feel I belonged in the 'inner circle' of a circuit overseer and his wife. Since the host couple were running back and forth, to and from the kitchen, it was hard to include them in the dinner conversation. It was an awkward situation ... and about to get worse.

As the meal proceeded, the conversation deteriorated into the circuit overseer telling jokes and cracking one-liners. When the jokes were not appropriate for the ears of our hosts, he switched from speaking French to speaking English. Gradually, he began to make hushed, 'humorous' remarks about the home and the possible source of the food we were being served ... in English. While we were aghast that someone who claimed to represent Jehovah and the Watchtower Society could be so insensitive, the things he said were so 'off the wall' funny, that at times we did not succeed at suppressing our laughter. I recall choking at one point when I was trying to swallow food and stifle a laugh at the same time.

It was the most bizarre feeling to be shocked, embarrassed and ashamed of what was happening at the table, and still to find myself unable to contain my giggles. At one point Terry said something like "*Okay, guys this is going too far*" but the circuit overseer just kept the wildly funny but inappropriate cracks coming ... making me wonder now, if we were drinking wine with the meal. The combination of his cutting wit, our embarrassment, and the tension in the room had us sniggering in spite of our distaste for what was happening. Fortunately, the only way the circuit overseer was expecting us to participate in dehumanizing this couple was by laughing.

The worst part of the whole debacle was that I later wondered if the garbage man husband could understand English (perhaps even speak it), because I remembered the little town where he was the garbage collector was an English-speaking enclave. Had he understood every rude remark of the circuit overseer? Had he realized exactly what we were giggling and laughing about? In Terry's and my defense I have to say that there were many jokes at which we managed not to laugh and no derisive wit came out of our mouths. (Some of the cracking-up was, of course, a physical release of the incredible tension we were feeling in this awful situation.)

I still wince when I recall that evening. My snickering was bad enough, but what that circuit overseer did was despicable. While there is no excuse for our participation in that tawdry affair, I have to say that Terry and I were well-indoctrinated in the rules of the JW hierarchy and did not feel comfortable contradicting or challenging a circuit overseer. Due to that subtle indoctrination about levels of power in the organization, we allowed ourselves to participate in a callous, cruel scenario. I would never have dreamed that one of the most shameful acts of my life would have been in the company of, and instigated by a circuit overseer. I have wondered if the circuit overseer had been even more sinister, would we have been able to stand up against him and say *"This is not right and we will not participate!"*? Of course, I would like to think so, but we all know of examples throughout history where seemingly good people went against their own values and engaged in heinous activities.

Over and over I saw examples of how the values and principles we Witnesses claimed to espouse were not the ones that we were able to live. Seeing these many failures of ethical, kind and decent behavior (some my own) was another factor in dissolving my trust that this was *"the truth"*. While many of the Watchtower expectations were stringent and stifling, others were common social norms that people claiming to adhere to Bible principles, like ourselves, should have been able to follow. There were, unfortunately, many examples of undue influence, acting out, and reprehensible behavior. It was hard to equate these examples of unethical behavior (including my own) with the high ideals of behaviour we were expected to uphold ... and told the public we upheld.

"We keep on being told that religion, whatever its imperfections, at least instills morality. On every side, there is conclusive evidence that the contrary is the case and that faith causes people to be more mean, more selfish, and perhaps above all, more stupid." ~Christopher Hitchens

"The disappearance of a sense of responsibility is the most far-reaching consequence of submission to authority." ~Stanley Milgram

CHAPTER 26

Gentlemen Prefer Blondes

A friend (our former housemate from the little house on the hill), and I went to choose the lining for a fur coat she was having made. She wanted my opinion about the choices of colors and patterns for the lining of the new coat. The owner of the fur store, Mr. Mayer (not his real name) was a large, cigar-smoking man with tobacco-stained fingers. He was a multi-lingual, master-salesman millionaire.

While my friend mulled over the lining material options for her coat, Mr. Mayer urged me to try on some of the luxurious furs in his showroom. I did. They felt dreamy and looked good. There was no public awareness back then about the obscenity of killing animals for their fur, when there are other options for clothing. P.E.T.A. (People for the Ethical Treatment of Animals) did not yet exist to help raise awareness. So my friend had no guilt attending the purchase of her fur coat and I had no qualms about trying them on and fantasizing about having one. Bitterly cold winters in Quebec seemed to make fur coats a 'must have' back then.

Mr. Mayer said if I would like a fur coat, he would make me a really good deal. I told him I could not direct any of our income toward the purchase of a fur coat. He raised an eyebrow, and said, *"What does your husband do?"*

I told him what we both did in terms I hoped he could understand. It looked like he understood very well what Jehovah's Witnesses 'do'. He came very close to rolling his eyes in disgust, leaving me with the impression that he already had some strong opinions about the sect.

After my friend selected the material for her coat lining and wrote a cheque to pay for it, Mr. Mayer inquired if I knew how to do any bookkeeping. I replied in the affirmative. *"Well I need a bookkeeper"*, he said. *"Come work for me and I'll have the men upstairs make you whatever kind of fur coat you want. You can pay it off weekly with a part of your salary."*

My friend jokingly bristled and said, *"You didn't make me that kind of offer!"* Mayer didn't miss a beat and replied, *"You're not blonde!"*

I didn't know how to reply to this offer of a job (and a fur coat!). Surely he wanted someone to work full-time and would take back his offer once he realized I could only work part-time. But a part-time bookkeeper was what he said he wanted and before long I was spending every Friday sitting across from the millionaire, transposing numbers from sales receipts into his general ledger, breathing in cigar smoke, and ... sporting a beautiful, new fur coat.

While Mr. Mayer was always proper and respectful with me, it was evident that he did have a thing for blondes. His wife had a head of extravagantly long, bleached, blonde hair. He told me he had met her in Israel and brought her back to Canada to be his wife. (When I think back on the two of them now, it occurs to me that their relationship might be compared to the one in the old movie "Pretty Woman" with Julia Roberts and Richard Gere.) They had a sweet, if demanding, little blonde daughter, too. (I suspected that the child's hair was also bleached to achieve its platinum tone.) One afternoon as he sat across the desk from me and was in a talkative mood, Mayer told me this story that I recount now to the best of my memory:

Apparently I wasn't the first young blonde Jehovah's Witness to whom Mayer had offered a job. Fifteen years earlier he had noticed a young, blonde woman standing every weekday morning between 8:00 a.m. and 9:00 a.m. at the same street corner with the Watchtower and Awake! Magazines. He quickly figured out she was a Jehovah's Witness. He felt sorry for her, as he rarely saw anyone approach her or buy her magazines. He decided one day while driving to work that he would stop and buy the girl's magazines just to encourage her and put a smile on her face. He did, and promptly threw them in the garbage when he arrived at his store. He always nodded to her as he drove by her street corner and once he figured out that the magazines were issued bi-weekly, he decided to stop every second week and purchase them - *"just to help her out"*. He never had an iota of interest in reading them. This pattern went on for a few months. They developed a friendly repartée in their regular but brief conversations.

One day, when it was particularly cold he persuaded her to let him buy her a cup of coffee in a nearby restaurant. Over coffee he tried to convince her that she should not stoop to standing on the street corner selling magazines. It was beneath her, he said. No woman should hang out on the street corner like that. She could be doing better things with her life.

His arguments to get her off the street (including offering her a job) did not work, but she did see he was no threat, meant well, and she occasionally accepted other invitations for coffee. He said he grew to care for her over those cups of coffee and at one point he again begged her to get off the street corner for good, to get out of that silly religion and make a real life for herself. This time, he told her he would help her to do just that - he would take care of her. He would take care of *everything* for her. He assured her he would ask *nothing* of her in return. All he wanted was for her to get off of the street, quit being a Jehovah's Witness, and he would take care of everything else. He thought he had made an offer that would be impossible for her to refuse. She was, however, immovable - from the both the street corner and from the religion.

Mr. Mayer claimed, during our conversation, that the fact she was so blindly loyal to the Jehovah's Witnesses and refused his offer, broke his heart. He must have ended the story there as I don't recall him saying what ultimately became of her, or their friendship.

I later made inquiries in the congregation to see if anyone could recall a young blonde pioneer from fifteen or so years previous, who had the habit of standing in the early morning with the magazines at the corner of the city's main streets - to no avail.

Now the story of the furrier and the blonde is just as I remember Mr. Mayer telling it, and of course, it has always been begging for further interpretation. Was there ever a young, blonde JW standing on the street corner? Had Mayer really made her the offer to take care of her if she would abandon being a Jehovah's Witness? Or ... was Mayer perhaps testing or baiting me with this story to see what my response would be? Your guess is as good as mine. I prefer to think that Mayer's story was true, unfolded just as he described it, and was not some elaborate 'come-on'. My husband, however, has always insisted that Mayer manufactured the story in a stealth attempt to add another filly to his fair-haired stable.

I am more partial to believe the story as Mayer told it, but then again I was carefully trained to take everything literally and at face value by the Watchtower organization. Why start to infer hidden meaning when it was not my wont? Perhaps the best way of not having to deal with a possible cryptic, veiled proposition was to pretend I just didn't get it. A dumb-blonde gambit, one could say.

A great hope fell
You heard no noise
The ruin was within.
~Emily Dickinson

CHAPTER 27

The Need is Great

Terry and I continued to be special pioneers for about five years. He was the presiding overseer for the French-speaking congregation in Sherbrooke during that time. It was in the late sixties that the Governing Body claimed that research into Bible chronology linked to the time of the end, indicated the Great Tribulation leading to the Battle of Armageddon would begin in 1975. They then began to publish articles in the Watchtower magazine encouraging members to intensify their efforts in the preaching work. Lives were at stake! As 1975 approached, JWs were exhorted to consider serving as full-time servants, where the need was great. A Kingdom Ministry, published in May, 1974 said, "*Yes, the end of this system is so very near! Reports are heard of brothers selling their homes and property and planning to finish out the rest of their days in this old system in the pioneer service. Certainly this is a fine way to spend the short time remaining before the wicked world's end.*" Imagine all the brothers and sisters who dutifully took heed!

The Governing Body went so far as to make suggestions that could affect every facet of a JW's life. For example, they would say things like: "*With the end so close, would lovers of Jehovah want to invest their energies into getting an education, building a business, buying a house, etc. or would they recognize that now is the time to consider full-time service?*" They rarely made explicit orders. Rather, they would wrap what they wanted members to do, in innocent-sounding questions to which the only response was the one they wanted, or by citing supposed 'examples' from letters to the Watchtower revealing what *"some devoted brothers and sisters are already doing"* – the implication being - *"what you, too, should be doing".*

Soon after these suggestions with regard to 1975 appeared in JW literature, a family (mother, father and two teenage boys) from Western Canada arrived in our town in Quebec. They wanted to learn French and serve as pioneers in our congregation. This brother had quit a management job, sold their home, removed their boys from their schools, totally uprooting his family because he believed the end was about to arrive. They made huge sacrifices to follow the Watchtower's exhortations to serve where the need was great.

Fine people like this family gave up their homes, gave up life insurance and gave up future pensions on the belief that they could trust what the Governing Body said. I felt rather sorry for the mother in this family. I suspect she was never as convinced as her husband that they should have effected such drastic changes on the basis of Watchtower's new chronology.

The two teenage boys of this couple must have also experienced the pressure of bizarre reassurances like this one in the May 22, 1969 AWAKE! Magazine, *"If you are a young person, you also need to face the fact that you will never grow old in this present system of things. Why not? Because all the evidence in fulfillment of Bible prophecy indicates that this corrupt system is due to end in a few years."* Those two teenagers would be in their mid-fifties now. The Governing Body prepared JWs to make those sort of major sacrifices, always accentuating that they, the GB, were direct representatives of God on earth. They claimed everything they wrote in their literature was inspired by God. I often think of some of the JWs we knew who made such huge lifestyle sacrifices - wondering how their lives unfolded when the end never came. Apparently many left the religion after 1975 because of feeling so cavalierly misled.

It's difficult to understand the hubris of a leadership that interfered so callously in the lives of their followers. But we, the *"sheep"* as we were called, had been trained to follow their pronouncements … to the detriment of our lives, relationships and well-being. Had we had any idea of the extent of the exploitation, things may have turned out very differently for everyone.

CHAPTER 28

Manipulation & Exploitation

Of course, there was as much method as madness to the ways the WBTS manipulated and exploited their adepts. It's my contention that once the organization had a more business-minded president, Nathan H. Knorr, it began to operate like a pyramid scheme. Multi-level marketing schemes accrue profits based mainly on *the number of people they can recruit. Recruits are required to buy the products they sell*. Multi-level marketing plans need to have a good product to sell. The profits are made by attracting more and more people to join the scheme and purchase the products themselves, to then use to recruit more people, ad infinitum.

In the case of the Watchtower Bible & Tract Society, the Bible-based, doomsday dogma in their literature was their product. The meetings were their sales training sessions. The 'publishers' were the sales force sent out to attract more recruits who would also need to purchase literature to sell. Part of the 'religious indoctrination' given to the eager sales force was that the end of times was nigh and people must be warned about their imminent destruction – unless they, too, become converts/recruits. Lives were at stake, including our own. Incentives to witness, publish, convert or recruit were, thereby, always framed with urgency.

The truth is, that back when I was a young *"publisher"* the WBTS made some of its vast wealth from the monies paid by the publishers themselves to stock their book bags with Watchtower publications for this urgent sales promotion work. Once the publishers had purchased millions upon millions of newly released publications for a small fee, the corporation was already making large profits. Then it required us to use what we had purchased to try and lure in more recruits who would also purchase and sell Watchtower's printed products.

The WBTS did not ask us to remit whatever monies we received from householders who purchased the Bibles, books or magazines. All they needed to make money were the pennies we paid them for multiple copies of each publication, and then more and more recruits to purchase more and more publications. So yes, back then the real customers of this mega printing operation were Jehovah's Witnesses themselves. At weekly sales meetings we would replenish our personal stock of magazines and books before going out in local neighborhoods looking for new recruits. We paid between one third and one half of what we charged the person at the door. The pennies we gained did not enrich any of us, as we had to pay for our gasoline to get to the assigned territory and were never paid a cent for the time we devoted to going door-to-door. Truth be told, very few householders were interested in purchasing the literature anyway.

Not only were we the real customers of the WBTS, some among us were recruited to offer our time and energy *at no charge*, to work in their printing plants to produce the literature the rest of us would then have to buy. On top of that, we were expected to make monetary contributions (donations) to the organization to further the "*kingdom preaching work*" around the globe.

We were told that if we could not sell the magazines (they actually used the word "*place*" the magazines, so we could avoid thinking of ourselves as salespersons and fool ourselves into thinking we were servants of Jehovah), we should give them away before the next issue was published. We left unsold copies in waiting rooms, bus stations, laundromats, etc. so people could supposedly read about the good news of God's kingdom. The WBTS actually did not really care if magazines we had purchased were given away or even read, as they had already made their money on these magazines when their loyal sales force paid for them at the Kingdom Hall.

With this clever marketing scheme, The Watchtower Bible and Tract Society developed an international printing business with branches and printing plants in many countries around the world. The headquarters was in Brooklyn, New York where their printing operation and residences for all the volunteer workers took up several blocks of valuable real-estate. This real-estate has since appreciated greatly and is worth multi-millions, if not billions. No doubt other high-return investments were made with all the money that rolled in.

Some meetings of Jehovah's Witnesses were built around studying the religious literature printed in these plants, so each Witness, including all children, were encouraged to have their own copies of books and magazines for study and meetings, as well as the copies they hoped to sell in their preaching work. These millions of personal copies were also paid for. My mother (often on welfare at the time) would purchase thirty to forty copies of each issue of the Watchtower and Awake! Magazines. She also purchased multiple copies of every book they ever printed. Multiply similar purchases by millions of other devoted servants across the globe!

The WBTS got the Witnesses to devote their lives in service to the organization and to work for free to print, purchase and then sell their literature. The plan worked for decades. Since the Watchtower works hard to be classified as a religion in every country in which they operate, they payed no sales tax on the sales of printed matter, nor income tax on their profits, nor property tax on their significant property holdings throughout the world. In recent years the WBTS has had to stop charging the public for their literature due to concerns they would lose their classification as a religion and, thereby, have to pay both income taxes as well as property taxes on their billions in property holdings. In truth, the WBTS has led its followers, the public and the governmental authorities into believing it is a religion when it is in fact a very clever multi-marketing scheme and real-estate conglomerate. As Eric Hoffer said, *"Every great cause begins as a movement, becomes a business, and eventually degenerates into a racket."* Perhaps Hoffer was just echoing what Judge Rutherford said back in 1939: *"Religion is a snare and a racket."* Of course, Rutherford claimed he was referring to *other* religions, but we all know how easily projection can sneak into much of what we say.

What is particularly galling to me about what the WBTS did back then, was how they accentuated that the preaching work was an essential part of our worship of God and that the literature was a key instrument from Jehovah to alert the nations that He would soon intervene in human affairs and destroy the wicked at his Battle of Armageddon. There was always an urgency attached to the preaching work. People had to know how to save themselves from imminent destruction! We were doing God-ordained, life-saving work *and had to purchase the literature that we would offer to people*, to literally save their lives! In fact, whenever sales of the magazines seem to slump, it seemed the WBTS top brass would come up with a new, soon-to-arrive date for Armageddon, or a special sales campaign in order to add to the urgency of the preaching work and incite the devoted publishers to work even harder, buy more and increase sales. When new dates for the end were announced they then pushed for followers to literally pick up stakes and move to "*serve full-time where the need was great*". Many devoted JWs gave up homes, jobs, lives and moved to obey these urgent calls to save as many lives as possible from destruction at Armageddon. Of course, once working all day, every day in the field service, rank and file would need to purchase many more copies of the magazines than before. The Watchtower of March 15, 1969, p. 171 says, "*This world has very little time left! Any 'future' this world offers is no future! Wisely, then, let God's Word influence you in selecting a course that will result in your protection and blessing. Make pioneer service, the full-time ministry, with the possibility of Bethel or missionary service your goal.*" Even missionaries and full-time servants of the organization had to pay for the literature they were going to sell from door-to-door.

At the same time, the organization knew that very few people actually became Jehovah's Witnesses because of buying a magazine or book from the Witnesses in this bogus, unrelenting door-to-door preaching work. Most people who converted to become Jehovah's Witnesses were relatives, friends, neighbors or co-workers of a current JW. All this frenzied activity of going door-to-door before Armageddon, was really just to get us to fill our briefcases full of purchased books and magazines. Governing body members knew all that door-to-door work produced very few converts. In his book, "In Search of Christian Freedom", Raymond Franz says: "*In reality, there is strong evidence that only a **minority** of Witnesses became such as the result of a visit to their doors. I have asked groups of persons by what means they became Witnesses and, in each case, out of perhaps a dozen persons only one or two had first been interested through that means. The **majority** were interested by family members,*

workmates, acquaintances and similar contacts. Reports by circuit overseers have presented similar evidence. One of the elders quoted ... stated, 'In more and more territories it seems increasingly clear that most of the increase is coming from informal witnessing efforts rather than from door to door.'" (Page 221, footnote) So the Watchtower's crafty manipulation was to make us believe we were doing God's end of days warning work and fool the ever-growing number of recruits into being the actual customers of their books, Bibles and magazines. It was a misleading multi-marketing scheme telling us that we needed to get God's message to the masses via their religious literature and via the door-to-door ministry, in order to save lives.

To summarize:

- All JW rank and file production and preaching services were given freely to The Watchtower Corporation.
- Rank and file had quotas of hours they should spend each week in the house-to-house preaching work. Knowing they were expected to spend several hours each week in this "service", they had to be prepared by having purchased several copies of the magazines and books in order to offer them to the general public - the supposed customer.
- The WBTS dates for the Battle of Armageddon were always being updated to lend a never ending urgency to the preaching work.
- As devoted members of the organization, we paid small amounts regularly for millions upon millions of publications we were told God wanted us to distribute to the doomed masses of humanity.
- **None of our door-to-door work really counted for anything, as the WBTS knew the house-to-house work drew few converts (which they claimed was what they wanted and what would result).** Their primary goal was for more and more active publishers to buy millions of magazines and books.
- The Watchtower, Bible and Tract Society became a multi-national printing company (while claiming to be a religion) with this secret marketing scheme. JWs themselves were unknowingly the real customers for the Watchtower Corporation. **Jehovah's Witnesses themselves bought the magazines and that was what created the growth of this huge printing conglomerate.** It did not matter one iota whether the

public bought the magazines from us or not. The organization made monumental profits with their growing number of adherents as their customers.
- The organization **had a guaranteed base of customers who bought several copies of every item they produced**. They clearly understood and used the concept of volume sales for low prices as another facet of their marketing scheme which exploited their own devoted followers.
- The Watchtower Bible & Tract Society has, therefore, made itself a multi-billion dollar publishing corporation by exploiting their own loyal followers. As the money rolled in during the middle and latter half of the twentieth century, the corporation invested these millions in profits in valuable properties across the globe. Claiming to be a religion allowed (and still allows) them to be exempt from paying sales tax, income tax, property tax and/or school taxes in the places where they acquired property and built satellite printing plants. As Scientology founder, L. Ron Hubbard said, "*If you want to get rich, you start a religion.*"

Of course, times have changed. More and more people now prefer to get their information digitally rather than in print form. Governments are keeping a close eye on so-called religious, non-profit organizations. The Watchtower's multi-marketing scheme seems to have collapsed right out from under them. This has required the WBTS to rebrand themselves as JW.ORG and to revamp their corporate strategies, sales procedures and money-making practices in order to retain their tax exempt status. Rank and file now offer the literature for free to the public. They also use custom-designed carts to display the free literature on street corners. Congregations must pay the Watchtower Society for these thousands of display carts.

Of late JW.ORG has even been reduced to asking for donations of insurance policies, stock dividends, gold jewellery, real-estate, real-estate income, and even to be made the sole recipients of JW members' wills. All this because they have had to both reduce the amount of literature they produce, and stop charging for it for fear they would lose their tax-exempt status. This has recently necessitated a lot of downsizing in the organization. JW.ORG now reaches out to members to share their dogma and request donations using videos, cartoons and their new JW Broadcasting platform. It is difficult now to distinguish the Watchtower Society from your everyday fundamentalist tel-evangelists. Nathan Knorr and Fred Franz must be rolling over in their graves ... squirming on their thrones ... or whatever!

How many of us spent our young lives engaged in the Watchtower organization's bogus Kingdom Ministry work? What a monumental deception and waste of our life energy and limited time on this planet. This corporation, masquerading as a religion, has not limited its deceptions to the above examples. Their deceptions are rife and you can find tons of damning evidence of their 'high crimes and misdemeanors' with the tip of your fingers by doing simple Google searches. The Watchtower commandeered our goodwill, robbed us of our youth, time, energies, ability to dream, ability to choose, personal goals, in some cases our health, while in other cases our very lives. It always baffles me why, with all the evidence available, that some ex-JWs struggle to name this organization for what it is ... a cunning corporate cult masquerading as a religion.

*"... whether greed or God is the currency,
it is not right to own another's free agency."*
~Rebecca Musser

*"Go to your bosom:
Knock there,
And ask your heart
What it doth know."*
~Shakespeare

CHAPTER 29

Are You Happy?

During our time special pioneering, back problems started up again. I was finding it hard to sit through two hour meetings. The discomfort made me edgy and nervous - sometimes feeling like I wanted to jump right out of my skin. A kind, older sister pioneering with her husband in a town near Sherbrooke recommended a good chiropractor.

As special pioneers we had no health insurance but decided that a few treatments with this recommended clinician might be just what I needed. We drove to the neighboring town where this chiropractor was located. As any ethical practitioner should, he conducted a brief interview to create a file with my medical history. After I described the history of past and current physical symptoms the conversation continued something like this:

Doctor: *And what is it you do for a living?*
Me: *I'm a full-time representative for Jehovah's Witnesses - kind of a missionary, I guess.*
Doctor: *What does that involve?*
Me: *Well, I go door-to-door looking for people who would like to study the Bible.*
Doctor: *And are you successful?*
Me: *Depends on what you mean by "successful", but yes we do find people who want to study the Bible with us.*
Doctor: *And are you happy doing this?*
Me: *Yes, of course.*
Doctor: *From what you have already told me about your symptoms, I would say that your body does not sound very happy ... Have you ever considered that your physical pain could have something to do with your choice of vocation?*

Me: ... silence ... (I had no idea how to respond to his comment and question. My conscious mind was trying to process what he meant, while my subconscious was desperately trying to keep me from really hearing the truth I already knew in the statement.) I could not, and did not respond ...

Doctor: *Sometimes our comfort level in our body is a good indicator of our comfort level in the life we have created for ourselves. I have a strong sense that if you reconsidered how you use your life energy, that your back discomfort would disappear and you would feel much better.*

Me: ... *I'm here to get a treatment for my back problem, not to have you tell me how to lead my life!*

He had voiced what I knew in my heart of hearts to be true - but it was not a truth I could allow myself to entertain. Hearing someone articulate the truth of my life made me confused, angry and upset. I was not able to reflect any more deeply than that.

This chiropractor had tickled the truth that I worked so hard to suppress and I burst into tears and ran out of his office, without ever getting the treatment. I rushed to the parking lot where Terry waited in the car. Terry must have thought I'd been molested by the chiropractor as I ran red-faced and crying toward him, but the good doctor had merely spoken the truth. Truth I was not able to fully grasp at that time.

We drove home while shaking our heads about what a 'know-nothing' that chiropractor was. I tried to put the incident and all of its implications out of my mind, but somewhere it had all been recorded and put on file in my subconscious. The brutal truth waited for a later time when I would have the maturity and strength to address it.

For now the implications of recognizing the truth of my existence just seemed too great. If I admitted what I knew to be true, changes would have to be made. Terry did not view "*the truth*" and "*the work*" the way I did. The only relative I had who was not in the truth was my father and I had no idea where he was or if he was even still alive. I felt totally alone in my malaise and totally unequipped to face the decisions I needed to make.

Trappist monk, Thomas Keating says that life calls us to attain a level of "*maturity we are not capable of if all we have is blind faith and literalism.*" I certainly did not have the maturity or courage to reconsider and possibly reject everything about my life. It just seemed impossible at that time. Also due to my many nagging physical problems (which I understand now were a direct result of systemic changes in my body due to all the stress and adversity of being a Witness) I did not have the emotional or physical energy to advocate on my own behalf. It would be challenging enough to walk away from your life if you were in good health. To contemplate such a huge undertaking when you are always battling some sort of chronic fatigue, physical pain. or perplexing illness was beyond daunting.

"Breaking free is only the beginning. Then begins the painful process of reversing the indoctrination. The longer someone stays in a cult the harder it is for them to remember who they were before the cult took control of their mind. Or in the case of someone like me, a cult-born child, my entire personality was made and created by them. When I left I had no idea who I was. My whole existence, everything I thought I knew, had been a lie."
~Natacha Tormey,
Born into the *"Children of God"* cult.

Be crumbled.
So wild flowers will come up where you are.
You have been stony for too many years.
Try something different.
Surrender.
~Rumi

CHAPTER 30

Circuit Work or Baby?

After a visit of a circuit overseer to our congregation (not the flirty one or the joking one) Terry told me that he was being recommended for circuit work. In circuit work he would be a travelling elder with approximately twenty congregations that he would visit for a week at a time, assessing each congregation's spiritual health. His job would be to encourage the brothers and help the elders with any congregational problems. At that time, any couples who went into circuit work, had to give up having a home of their own. (Some fortunate circuit overseers and their wives got a home base such as a little apartment in the basement or attic of a Jehovah's Witness home or Kingdom Hall - but I was not aware of anything like that in Quebec at that time.) We would have had to live each week out of a suitcase in a room provided in a local JW home for the duration of the visit with the congregation. Every meal except breakfast would be at a different Witness home. Each Witness family considered it an honor to receive the circuit overseer and his wife for a meal and would work hard, make sacrifices and prepare something special for them. In return, they rightly expected the circuit couple to be upbeat, bright, interested and attentive. Circuit overseers and their wives were always expected to be available, 'on' and encouraging.

That's well and good, but day after day it must be incredibly taxing and wearisome. The wives of circuit overseers simply followed their husband, participated in field service and were expected to be as encouraging as possible to the sisters in the congregation. Any free hours during the week were spent in someone else's home. That was their life. That was it. Circuit overseers' wives owned nothing, decided nothing, had no home, no prospects of one and few personal possessions. Why they did not even have a room, bathroom or bed of their own!

Secretly I was not especially keen to follow my husband into circuit work. Of course I had been encouraged to believe it was a privilege (any work the Watchtower organization asks you to do is called a *'privilege'*) but deep down I knew otherwise. Terry had, however, worked long and hard in the Watchtower trenches and it would be nice for him to move up in the male JW hierarchy. Terry was ready for new and more challenging responsibilities. It would be a position he would be very good at. How could I tell him it was not for me? Terry said it was just a recommendation and might never happen, or might only happen down the road as the recommendation could just sit in the Toronto Bethel files. He suggested that we should not wonder too much about it for the moment.

We went on holiday to Prince Edward Island using a camper trailer lent to us by Terry's parents. During our vacation I experienced bouts of serious nausea and we became suspicious that I was pregnant. Upon returning home, a letter from Toronto Bethel awaited us. Our presence was requested at Toronto Bethel so Terry could begin circuit training. Eek! I made an immediate appointment with an obstetrician and my pregnancy was confirmed. Terry was wonderfully upbeat and excited about the pregnancy, but I knew some part of him must have also been disappointed to be on the verge of attaining a long time goal, and have it snatched away.

Terry had to return the camper trailer to his parents in Ontario and would stop at Toronto Bethel to let them know he was no longer a candidate for circuit work. I saw him off and then walked to the grocery store to restock our empty cupboards. I couldn't help it - I was so happy. I felt as if I could float up off of the sidewalk with sheer delight! A baby! And ... phew, no circuit work. I was both excited and relieved.

The pregnancy was a difficult one. I had morning sickness that lasted all day, every day, for months (Hyperemesis Gravid Arum). I lost twelve pounds during those first months of pregnancy and was hospitalized twice for intravenous rehydration. Looking back now, I have to wonder if the pregnancy became a high risk one because of all the stress chemicals floating around in my system and wreaking havoc with my well-being due to the stress of being raised in a dysfunctional household and so unhappy as a Jehovah's Witness.

Now I have to admit as difficult as those months were, there was a secondary gain. I missed many meetings and a lot of field service because of being so sick. It was a nice change, when not hanging over the toilet, to have some time to myself - time to think and time to plan for the arrival of a new life. As the birth approached we both quit pioneering. Terry found a full-time job as a graphic artist and we began to set up a real home for our little family. Was it possible that we might finally begin to live a simple, normal life?

The due date for the birth came and went and my doctor became concerned that my mounting blood-pressure was an indication of "pre-eclampsia" which is dangerous for both mother and baby. Terry, as usual, was scheduled to give the Memorial talk that spring and I kept asking him to please find someone else to give it. I had a suspicion that the baby would be born on the night of the full moon (it is, of course, always a full moon on Memorial night). I desperately wanted him by my side during the birth. He didn't think that it was very likely that our baby's birth and the Memorial would happen on the same night and, for a while, resisted my request. Eventually he asked another brother to give the Memorial talk, "*just in case*".

We had a beautiful baby girl born at around 9:30 p.m. on the night of the full moon – Memorial night. Had Terry not asked another brother to give the Memorial talk, he would have been overseeing the passing of the emblems around the congregation while I was in the last and worst part of the labor. I was so grateful to have him with me throughout the labor and delivery of our first child. There were complications with the delivery and while the baby was fine, I needed to be monitored and was kept in hospital for nine days. We named our baby Taira (a combination of my husband's name and my mother's name). The name is pronounced like every other Tara, we just felt the need to complicate it with an extra vowel. Taira frequently 'thanks' us for that.

A few weeks after the birth, Terry's mother came to spend a few days with us and meet her new granddaughter. Our relationship had not changed much from the time of our first meeting. It was still not good. Of course every first-time grandmother is enchanted with the new addition to the family, and that was certainly the case for Terry's mother, Eloise.

One day of her visit, just after our evening meal, Eloise announced that she would take care of the baby while we both went to the Ministry School and Service Meeting. I had not planned on going to those meetings and told her the baby was due for a feeding during that time anyway. I had had a difficult labor and birth. (In fact, I later had to have two operations to try and correct the damage from a botched episiotomy.) Terry's mother knew I was still recuperating, weak, and breast-feeding. When she made the announcement that I would attend the meeting and she would care for Taira, she had our baby in her arms. Each time that I approached to take my newborn, Eloise turned away and would not let me have her. Terry could sense that a tense and possibly explosive situation was brewing between his wife and his mother and tried to find a way to de-escalate the tension. He finally whispered to me that his mother would only be with us for another day, and I should perhaps just take this opportunity to get out, away from her, and to go to a meeting with him ... that maybe it would do me good.

I was furious at both of them. I cannot recall the exact words of the exchange with Eloise, but I had the distinct impression that whether or not I went to that meeting would be a measure of how good a Witness I was - or was not. I went to the bedroom and purposefully decided on a dress – a solid-colored, bright pink dress – and threw it on. When I went back to the living room I was still not able to get my baby back from Eloise. I would have had to wrestle or pry her away. I was not about to do that to my baby ... and was trying very hard not to let my already high stress-levels rise any higher. Trapped in this no-win situation, I finally said I would go to the meeting. However, I knew something that neither Terry nor his mother knew. I had a trump card up my sleeve.

The meeting began soon after our arrival, and we took our seats. I was not listening. I was still seething ... and waiting for what I knew would happen. Soon I started to feel a pins and needles sensation in my breasts. This is a signal that the "let-down reflex" is about to happen. The let-down reflex is also called the "milk ejection" process and in the first month of breast-feeding a newborn, the ejection of milk from the breasts can be powerful. The milk does not flow out of the breasts in little drips. The milk ejects in a straight, powerful spray. This reflex can be stimulated by the baby's cries, by full breasts, and even by a mother simply thinking about her baby.

I was thinking about how my baby had been commandeered by her grandmother and that normally about this time I would have been holding and feeding her. Suddenly my breasts started to spray out their contents. I decided to just sit there for a minute or two so Terry would have an undeniable 'visual' of how important and urgent it was for me to have our baby back in my arms. Once my solid pink dress had become saturated enough to make two huge, dark, dripping wet spots, I nudged him pointing to the undeniable evidence that I needed to be with our baby. He was aghast at what he saw and needed no further persuasion to get my coat to cover the soaked dress and drive me back home.

Once home we could hear our hungry baby crying and saw through the window that Eloise was walking back and forth in the living room trying to soothe her. I took off my coat and entered the room - breasts first. There was nothing to say to Eloise. She saw my soaked dress and immediately handed over the baby. Turning on my heel, I left the room to nurse Taira privately. Still angry about everything that had transpired, I retired with the baby without saying goodnight to her grandmother.

Somehow Eloise and I managed to be civil with each other until she left. There was something very wrong about pressuring a new mother to leave her newborn in order to attend a religious meeting. But in the skewed reasoning learned in the cult, JW meetings come before the needs of a mother and baby. There was no one, other than Terry, to whom I could speak about this. It would have been a sacrilege to utter critical thoughts aloud to a friend in the congregation about a devoted grandmother.

After his mother left, Terry apologetically reminded me that his mother had been raised by a harsh JW father who had his own mean streak that he often justified with scripture. Clearly Terry's mother had internalized the way she had been mistreated by her father and carried those wounds and behaviors into her way of acting in the world. Terry said his grandfather was well known for being authoritarian and mean-spirited even from the Kingdom Hall platform - often tearing a strip off of congregants that he felt were not measuring up to Watchtower standards. This kind of harsh behavior and parenting must also account for Uncle Art's mean-streak, exhibited at our wedding. Terry assured me that his mother was not mean or harsh with her three sons - she seemed to reserve that for the women who came along to steal their hearts.

Ten months after Taira's birth, we moved from Sherbrooke (the town where we worked as duped, full-time, unpaid volunteers for the Watchtower corporation) to the metropolis of Montreal. Montreal would be the city where we would both fade out of the cult – although neither of us knew this at the time of the move.

CHAPTER 31

How Much More?

As a new mother, and as a wife who finally had time and 'permission' to create a real home for her family, I resented having to drag my baby and myself out into the door-to-door ministry every week. Meetings were doable because I got to hold and cuddle Taira and could tune out from listening to the same old, same old lectures from the platform.

Terry was still an elder and was also the assembly overseer for our circuit of congregations. He was working full time at a new job in Montreal and he really had a plateful of responsibilities looking out for Watchtower Bible & Tract Society interests in our region. Good thing he was so competent and energetic. Terry gave a lot of public talks in other congregations around the city. Sometimes the baby and I accompanied him, sometimes not. I was really disenchanted with the organization by now and especially by the way it still gobbled up so much of our time, so whenever there was an opportunity to miss a meeting and do something interesting, I grabbed it.

Now that we had a baby I always found myself alone to look after her at the meetings and conventions. The Watchtower Society kept Terry too busy with his many responsibilities to even sit down in the audience and listen to the talks. I often wondered if he had really had to sit through them, as I did, (instead of running around behind the scenes working like a dog to organize things) if he, too, would have perhaps been bored, disenchanted and fed up. It seemed to me he was more involved with, and aware of, the procedures and policies of the organization than aware of the vapid content continually spewed from the platform. Perhaps that is why he often seemed baffled when I talked in a derogatory way about it all.

During the closing remarks at the end of one four-day District convention the brother at the podium said something to the effect: *"What will you be thinking about as you drive home and resume your life tonight? Will you be thinking of all the things you have to do next week? Will you be thinking of your upcoming vacation? Or will you, dear brothers and sisters, center your thoughts on all the wonderful spiritual food Jehovah has provided for you at this convention?"*

I was tired and those remarks just about had me blow a gasket. Of course, I sat there stone-faced but inside I was exploding, thinking: *"I sit here for four full days. I confine an active eighteen month old to three square feet around her chair for four days. I try to listen and look up Bible verses for four days. I have not done a thing I really want to do for four days, and that is still not enough for you! Now you (the organization) are* **telling us what to think on the way home in the car!** *Besides controlling every facet of my life for four days, you now want to control what goes on in my mind!"*

Of course that was not my only rant. There was a lot to rant about as an unhappy member of that repressive, controlling organization. Some of my favorite interferences to rant about at the time were:

- How the Governing Body, a group of unmarried, old men, (many of whom had lived in the sheltered, monastic, artificial, everything-provided-for-them-all-the-time environment of the Brooklyn Bethel their entire lives) tell couples how they could express themselves intimately with one another.
- How the Governing Body would presume to tell brothers what amount of hair they could have on their face, what color their shirts could be, how wide their ties could be, etc.
- How the Governing Body told sisters what length they should wear their skirts and that they could not wear slacks to the Kingdom Hall or in the field service.
- How the Governing Body suggested that a good Christian, when on vacation, would search out a Kingdom Hall and attend meetings while on holiday, too.
- How the Governing Body told us what kind of dances we could and couldn't do, what kind of music we could and couldn't listen to, what kind of films were and were not appropriate for viewing, etc. etc.

Terry usually listened silently as I ranted on about the audacity of the organization intruding into so many of our personal and private concerns. He sometimes defended the organization and even their unreasonable expectations. Mostly he just let me rant. But he was listening and quietly taking note. He just did not allow himself to get as upset or irritated by it all as I did, or he was much better than I at suppressing his irritation.

Ultimately what became most intolerable were the constant intrusions into the lives of we members of the sect. How dare they presume that they could interfere with our lives. I wanted to be independent, to think for myself, to explore and discover. I wanted to make my own choices and decisions and not be judged if I did not toe some arbitrary, limited, rinky-dink party-line. There was a glorious world out there with so much to be curious about. I was no longer willing to allow the Watchtower Society to bind my mind as Japanese women were required to bind their feet. If God existed, he had given me a mind that I was not going to allow to decompose listening to Watchtower's one-topic, one-note, dumbed-down palaver. No one still operating under their influence seemed to be able to understand this growing imperative inside me. The only one I ever dared share it with was Terry. He must have known, at this point, that I could not and would not take much more.

If you only knock long enough and loud enough at the gate, you are sure to wake up somebody.
~Longfellow

CHAPTER 32

Fred Franz

One summer while our daughter was barely a toddler, Terry's Uncle Art, the one who officiated at our wedding, called Terry to say that Brother Fred Franz, then vice-president of the WBTS, was making a special visit to the little town of Brockville, Ontario. Art *"just knew"* we would want to be there to meet Fred Franz in person, along with Branch Servant/Coordinator Ken Little and several other members of the Canadian headquarters. We went to hear Franz speak. There were so many things I would rather have been doing, but I again tried to be the 'supportive help-mate' I was supposed to be. I have no memory of the topic of the talk Brother Franz gave. It was easy to block him out because he gave such convoluted, rambling talks that were often impossible to follow and ultimately, boring. There were always more interesting things to contemplate.

Terry's Uncle Art made sure that several of us in attendance had the privilege of meeting Brother Franz. A pre-selected few 'privileged' attendees then had photographs taken with Brother Franz. One of the pictures taken was with our little daughter sitting on the knee of the brother who was behind the Watchtower declaration that the end would come in 1975, as well as all the intrusive orders about our personal lives and choices. Franz was kind and friendly to all of us who had been invited to meet him after the special talk including little Taira, who he rather awkwardly bounced on his knee while cameras clicked.

Rank and file members of Jehovah's Witnesses were not allowed to celebrate the birthdays of our children but we were allowed to celebrate and fawn over members of the Governing Body, as witnessed that day in Brockville. Uncle Art, who had cautioned me about behaviors that could be deemed as *"creature worship"* at our wedding, was clearly engaged in his own creature worshipping behaviors as he hovered around Fred Franz - trying to anticipate his every need and bring as many high-ranking Witnesses in attendance at the event into the vice-president's anointed presence. Notice that neither Terry nor I were invited to pose in photos *with* Fred Franz. That privilege was reserved for those with more rank than us, or for babies like Taira. Terry and I were expected to be thrilled just to be allowed to view 'the anointed presence' and attendant 'creature worship' from the sidelines.

Fred Franz, Vice President of the WBTS and Art Humphries, City Servant Toronto and Terry's uncle.

Glen How, Q.C., lawyer for WBTS in Canada; Ken Little, Canadian Branch Coordinator; Art Humphries, Toronto City Servant and Terry's uncle; and in front Fred Franz, V.P., WBTS. Photos taken after Franz's discourse in Brockville, Ontario, circa 1973.

Terry, Taira and I after the same special-member-of-the- governing-body-event in 1973 and in the same room as the above photographs. There was a photograph of Taira sitting on the knee of Fred Franz but it is nowhere to be found. I think in a fit of pique, during my exit from the cult, I tore it up.

By the way, Fred Franz's much-hyped 1975 came and went. Did he give any thought to the sacrifices millions of JWs made in anticipation of his so-called 'inspired' predictions? Did he ever apologize for those extreme sacrifices and the disappointments experienced by so many of the rank and file due to his faulty prediction? Not to my knowledge. In fact, in one convention talk after 1975 came and went, he actually blamed the brothers for any disappointment they experienced, saying that they had raised their expectations too high and wanted the end to come too much – or some malarkey to that effect. A blatant example of blaming the victims for the sacrifices they were urged to make and the disappointments and losses they suffered as a result.

Further, the Watchtower of July 15, 1976, p. 440 had the nerve to say that some of the rank and file *"...have planned their lives according to a mistaken view of just what was to happen on a certain date or in a certain year. They may have, for this reason, put off or neglected things that they otherwise would have cared for. But they have missed the point of the Bible's warnings concerning the end..."*

"Neglected things"? "Missed the point"? What a disingenuous display of rewriting history and shirking accountability after inciting thousands to give up jobs, cash out insurance policies, sell their homes and move at great expense to themselves and their families to serve where the need was great.

No wonder there was a huge out-flux of members in the years following another failed prophecy of the Governing Body. Twenty years later they suggested in the book, *"Proclaimers of God's Kingdom"* that the 1975 debacle resulted in a *"sifting out"* of those who were steadfast JW followers from those who weren't! What a perfect example of shaming, revisionist history by an always self-serving leadership.

But on that summer day of 1973 in Brockville, Ontario we got our fifteen minutes of basking in the anointed presence of the orchestrator of many of those debacles. How many more (now "over-lapping") generations of JWs will be disappointed by similar specious, fantasy predictions?

The world's flattery and hypocrisy
is a sweet morsel:
eat less of it ...
~Rumi

CHAPTER 33

Let Us Entertain You

Life moved along. As my frustration and discontent as a member of the sect grew, I did the minimum an elder's wife could do in the congregation without being reproved - probably creating a lot of consternation and gossip in our congregation and circuit. Terry had the opportunity to buy the business he worked for and though it was a huge undertaking with a lot of risk, he did it. This meant that he now was running a company with over thirty employees and still doing all the free volunteer work he did for the WBTS, not to mention the responsibilities that he had as a husband and father.

As our little girl got older there were expectations that we teach her all the Bible stories from the JW book designated for children at that time. I was very particular about what that innocent little mind of hers was exposed to on television. Why would I then expose her to ghastly images in Watchtower publications such as *My Book of Bible Stories* and *From Paradise Lost to Paradise Regained*, that would certainly trouble a little mind as much as a violent cartoon? I felt about Taira's mind as Mahatma Gandhi felt about his own: *"I will not let anyone walk through my mind with their dirty feet."*

JW children's books (filled with more and larger images than most Watchtower publications) contained all kinds of violent images that I did not want my daughter to view. No doubt they were written and illustrated by Bethel brothers who did not have children of their own. For example, the image of a father (Abraham) holding a knife above his son (Isaac) preparing to kill him and the graphic images of people fleeing, terrified of being destroyed by fire balls and cascading buildings at the Battle of Armageddon. What child needs to see the earth splitting apart ready to swallow up people that look just like their mommy and daddy? Suffice it to say, I refused to expose our daughter to those kind of age inappropriate, scary images. Since the "Kool-Aid" incident at a circuit assembly (Chapter 2), I was determined to not have our daughter immersed in JW doctrine nor be trained in blind obedience.

A circuit overseer and his wife (old friends of mine from Toronto days) let us know they would soon be in the Montreal area and hoped to visit us. Perhaps the gossip mill had alerted them about my diminishing loyalty to the organization and they wanted to see if they could help. We had not seen them for years as they had been busy working for the Watchtower organization in another part of the province. I was concerned about our ability to entertain them, as we now had a newborn who had a daily bout of colic (with attendant screeching and crying) at the supper hour. Terry said not to worry, that between the two of us we would make sure our old friends had a good time.

It was good to welcome Diane and David (not their real names) to our home after so many years. After a brief period of catching up with each other's lives, David turned his attention to our eldest daughter. He decided it would be great fun to test her on her knowledge of the Watchtower children's book, *My Book of Bible Stories*. All children love that! He urged her to go and find her copy so they could look at it together. My daughter did not have her own copy of the book and looked at her Dad and I with eyes questioning us as to what to do.

I was not pleased with David's stated intention to quiz our child and politely told him that we had never read to her from that book because the images were too violent and disturbing for little minds. Apparently no one had ever said that to him before. A look of surprise passed over David's face. I interpreted his cautiously critical expression to say, *"Well, this raises a few questions about you, Bonnie Zieman. What kind of a JW parent doesn't read to their child from the organization's 'Your Book of Bible Stories'?"* Everyone in the room now seemed a tad uncomfortable. What other things would arise in the conversation to reveal the disenchantment and looming defection of Sister Zieman?

Our evening together only proceeded from bad to worse. As we settled into our meal, Terry became unusually quiet and I noticed that his face took on a faint tinge of green. Suddenly he excused himself from the table and spent the rest of the evening retching in the bathroom upstairs. It was difficult to continue our meal and conversation knowing one of us was sick upstairs. Oh joy. Could this evening get any worse?

Soon our newborn awoke and was pumping her little legs with the pain of colic. I tried holding her tight and walking around the dining room while the circuit overseer and his wife did their best to finish their meal and converse. I could barely hear anything they said because of the baby's screams and knew that screaming was not the kind of background music that would help anyone's digestion. I decided the best thing to do was to remove myself and our screaming baby from the dining room and go downstairs. I made my apologies, asked them to please help themselves to anything they wanted, put a second bottle of wine on the table stating that if they didn't drink the wine with the meal to please take it home to help recover from this terrible evening.

Terry and I had discovered that one way to stop the baby's crying was to hold her tight while dancing vigorously to loud music with a good beat. So once downstairs I turned on Diana Ross singing "*upside down, boy, you turn me, inside out, and round and round ...*" and twirled around the play room. No doubt the pulsating beat throbbed the floor under the feet of Diane and David as the probably "*inappropriate*" lyrics wafted up the stairs.

So the circuit overseer and his wife sat alone at the dining room table while Terry had bouts of vomiting upstairs and I was dancing to Diana Ross downstairs. I don't remember whether Taira remained at the table with them or came downstairs with me. If she remained at the table with David and Diane, she was probably grilled about whether she knew the names of all the books of the Bible or all the names of the apostles (which she probably did not!). Diane and David finished their meal, and loaded the dirty dishes in the dishwasher before quietly leaving. Could we have *planned* a way to make guests feel any more uncomfortable? What a disaster!

Sometimes when I think back on that fiasco, I wonder if Terry's and my subconscious conspired to prevent that circuit overseer from ever delivering his intended (and uninvited and unwelcome) spiritual counsel to me. We've never had to absent ourselves like that, from guests in our home since!

A week later, the mailman delivered a large Hallmark card from Diane and David that said: **"WOW! WHAT A PARTY!"**

Apart from the dinner fiasco, something was made very clear that evening. The Watchtower Bible & Tract Society expected parents to be their surrogate indoctrinators-in-chief where children were concerned, at least until the Watchtower Society could step in and take over with even stronger mind-control techniques. Over the years I had submitted to so much indoctrination, but with the very marrow of my bones I knew that I *would not* be a party to the indoctrination or brainwashing of my children. I *would not* allow the Watchtower to impose on them what they had imposed on me. How could I expect of my children all the things that had caused me so much angst, confusion, shame and hurt? I could not, and would not.

For all those years, it seemed, I had not been able to summon the willpower to stand up on my own behalf. But now as a parent, I had the responsibility to protect my children from physical, emotional and spiritual harm. There was not a scintilla of hesitation to take on that task.

CHAPTER 34

Horny? ... Who Me?

When pregnant, Jehovah's Witness women have limited choices for their obstetricians. They must find one who is willing to attend the birth, however it unfolds, without the use of blood transfusions. So when we moved to Montreal, I took the referrals of some sisters in the city and saw an obstetrician who had already proved he was willing to work with JWs without using blood. (Mind you, once my first child was born I had made a secret decision that if ever my baby needed blood for a life-threatening condition, I would see to it that she received it. I was not going to prove *my* loyalty to Jehovah by sacrificing the lives of my children! I would assess whether or not to risk refusing blood for myself, as circumstances required.)

So I followed the sisters from our congregation to an obstetrician and he seemed perfectly ... adequate. During the ninth month of this third pregnancy I went in for what I hoped would be my last office visit and had to sit for quite a while in his waiting room ... as usual. Several other women waited there with me. Finally, once in his office, he told me that everything appeared to be fine and that we were now just waiting for the labor to begin. Then, leaning back in his chair, with a smirk on his face this doctor said:

Doctor: *You must be getting really horny by now.*
Me: *Pardon me?*
Doctor: *You must be feeling really horny by now.*
Me: *Oh, oh ... oh yes ... you wouldn't believe it! Why there was a woman sitting across from me in your waiting room chewing bubble gum with her mouth open. Her lips were all wet and gooey and she was making slurping*

and smacking sounds, blowing bubbles with her tongue and it was just driving me crazy!
Doctor: (silence and a confused look on his face) ... *Ah ... not sure we are talking about the same thing here ... anyway ... well ... moving right along ...*
I left the office and headed down to meet my husband who was parked close by. As we drove home, I casually asked Terry what the word "*horny*" meant.
Terry: *You don't know what the word "horny" means?!*
Me: *No ... not precisely.*
Terry: (smiling) *It means you are sexually excited - full of lust – ready to go - horny.*
Me: *What!!! If that's what it means how come I've never heard **you** use the word?*
Terry: *Well, I choose to express my lust for you in more 'well-bred' ways.*
Me: *Well, I wish you'd used the word 'horny' a time or two. Couldn't you just once have said, "Come here, woman. I'm horny?"*
Terry: *Why?*
Me: *Well the doctor just asked me if I was horny and I gave him a long, detailed description of how a woman in the waiting room, who was slurping, chewing and smacking her bubble gum, blowing bubbles using her tongue, and constantly licking her lips, was driving me crazy.*
Terry: *What!?*
Me: *I thought he was asking me if I'm feeling **irritable** in this last month of pregnancy!*
Terry & Me: an explosion of disbelief, embarrassment and laughter!

I include this silly story here, to show just how insulated, isolated and socially unaware Jehovah's Witnesses and even ex-Jehovah's Witnesses and can be. I bet even little, old Roman Catholic nuns know what the word "*horny*" means, but not this sheltered almost-ex JW girl, who didn't read trashy novels or see risqué movies. No. There I was thirty-one years old, pregnant with my third child, and my brain had never heard or registered the meaning of the word "*horny*".

Being raised with the isolation and naiveté of a Jehovah's Witness can result in many embarrassing situations out in the real world. I'm sure that sleazy doctor, who really should never have asked such an impertinent question, had fun telling that story in the ensuing years! Then again ... so have I!

Due to the information control and isolation imposed on Jehovah's Witnesses, those who leave the cult can expect to experience a period of feeling ill-equipped, out-of-sync, ignorant of so many normal things in, and ways of, the world. We emerge from the cult knowing little about politics, popular culture, science, rituals and celebrations, colloquial expressions, classic literature, music, finance, etc. When we leave the Watchtower organization we have to be prepared to negotiate a long and challenging learning curve.

    I eventually learned that rather than trying to hide how much I did not know about popular culture and/or politics, for example, in social situations when the conversation went beyond my scope of knowledge and comfort, and when appropriate, I simply said so. I disclosed that I had been raised in a high-control group and had been denied access to a lot of information, and participation in popular culture. I quickly learned to make jokes about my level of ignorance due to being raised in a cult. Laughter diffused the discomfort of both myself and the people around me about the gaps in my knowledge. I also asked people to help me understand more about the topic in question. I listened, learned, and asked a lot of questions. People love to share what they know, so most were pleased to help clue me in, and I slowly began to catch up with my peers.

CHAPTER 35

Options & Decisions

With the birth of a son, we found ourselves with three children, living in a suburb of Montreal and one of us, for all intents and purposes, out of "the truth". Our last two children were only twenty-two months apart in age so it was a very busy time for me with three children to care for. It was during this time of being busy with young ones that I really became totally inactive. Terry was now beginning to back off too and would soon be completely out. We did not write any letters of dissociation. We just tried to go about our lives without expectations or interference from any outside authority.

After a few years of grief-flavored freedom, I decided to take some courses in psychology at a community college. Looking back now, I know I took those courses as much to try to resolve my inner, JW-driven turmoil and neuroticism as to study the subject of psychology itself. Those basic courses led to enrolling in two therapy training programs - one in Gestalt therapy and then another called Psychosynthesis psychotherapy, which ultimately took four years of study and training. Those psychotherapy training programs hold that a good psychotherapist must do their own personal therapy, so while studying the theory and techniques to be a therapist, I had my own weekly, much-needed sessions with one.

A lot of my personal therapy centered around the repression of basic human needs, all the stolen hours, all the interference in my life, all the stress and anxiety, all the suppressed identity issues, and the shame I experienced being a Jehovah's Witness. The trainers and therapists with whom I worked really received a mini-education on the stultifying effects and inevitable wounds that can result from being raised in the Jehovah's Witness cult. The process of extricating your body, mind and spirit from the influence of the Watchtower Bible & Tract Society is difficult, but let me assure you it is definitely doable. There are thousands of examples to prove that assertion. I am but one.

Soon after, I applied to and was accepted at university studying in the Department of Applied Social Science of a sprawling, big-city university. Later a master's degree in education, (based on a thesis on adapting a model of experiential learning (Kolb) for use in conducting supervisions of student therapists) was earned. During several years of university study I learned much about the basic needs of humans and the damage that is done when those fundamental needs are thwarted. I studied the dynamics (needs and patterns) of people in group settings - which are really interesting to apply to the Jehovah's Witness organization. All the study and training explained much to me about my experience within the cult and certainly affirmed my hard-won decision to leave it.

In a course on Sociology, one of the books we were required to read was *"True Believer"* by Eric Hoffer. Hoffer was a brilliant longshoreman who became a renowned lay-sociologist. His seminal book shows how mass movements (of any kind) start and develop. I was flabbergasted at how Jehovah's Witnesses fit Hoffer's detailed profile of mass movements. Hoffer describes how mass movements persuade people to surrender their individuality in pursuit of a greater cause and how coercion is used to ensure the loyalty of their adepts. I was particularly interested in how Hoffer described that these idealistic movements inevitably morph into rule-laden institutions (businesses) consumed with making enough money to keep the organization growing. On the final exam, one of the questions gave students a choice of three topics on which to write a significant essay. One of the choices was *"Apply the principles of Hoffer's "True Believer" to a mass movement of your choice"*, or something to that effect. I jumped at that opportunity and poured everything I knew about Jehovah's Witnesses and how they specifically met the model in Hoffer's book, into my exam essay. Writing it was cathartic! I got an A+ and a note from the professor saying he had never seen a better application of *"True Believer"* to an actual group. I almost felt guilty taking credit for the essay – the fit of theory to the JW movement was SO perfect, and the writing of it was so easy and terrifically gratifying for a former Witness!

Of course I studied and learned the psychological theories, and trained in the therapeutic techniques that would allow me to eventually work as a psychotherapist and help others emerging from abusive or traumatic situations. Of the hundreds of people who were my clients, ultimately only two were Jehovah's Witnesses. I wish I could have helped more JWs and ex-JWs, but at that time I was not aware that many others were leaving the sect, nor did I see myself as any kind of 'expert' in exit-counselling. I was just happy to be out with my little family, to finally have access to an education and to create a professional life for myself with that education.

It took a while for my mother and my sister to realize that I had become more than just *"spiritually weak"*. They, like everyone else came to the only conclusion that made sense to them - that we must have succumbed to the dreaded lure of *"materialism"*. Terry was doing well in business and after years of living like paupers for the WBTS, we purchased a home, went on vacations, and dared to drive nice cars. This, people assumed, must be what drew us away from *"the truth"*. Of course, they had to protect themselves from the thought that former special pioneers and an elder could have seen major discrepancies in JW doctrine and practices which caused them to break away. Any material possessions and career opportunities we enjoyed could not compete with the simple yet profound satisfaction of being free.

Once my mother and sister figured out that I had made a deliberate decision to leave, they felt obliged to withdraw from me. They never asked any questions about my choice to leave. Wouldn't it be natural to want to ask *"Why?"* when a family member becomes inactive? They did not want to know why. Perhaps they were afraid they might be persuaded by my reasoning to walk away too. They never asked questions about what we did, what our interests were, where we went, who our friends were. As I shared some of the new things I was doing, they did not want to know any details about my education, my degrees, my work, my new offices, etc. When I told them a bit about any of these new learnings, activities or opportunities, it would just fall flat. They would never ask a follow-up question to understand more. They became people I did not know – distant, disinterested, insensitive and totally lacking in empathy – around me. The main topic of conversation was naturally the grandchildren and their activities. I was grateful we still, at least, had that interest in common! Mom talked about the health and goings-on of my aunts, uncles and cousins who were shunning me. Because the conversations became rather one-dimensional, the relationships devolved that way too. It was a sad, bittersweet and lonely time.

Sometimes we would talk about world events, but even that topic was a loaded one as they were dying to remind me that many of the events were sure signs that the end was near. I tried to help them feel comfortable about their JW activities by asking questions about the dates of assemblies, or about Mom's roles in an upcoming Biblical dramas, or the well-being of brothers and sisters I had known for years, etc. However, the schism created by one member of the family changing her mind about the organization was becoming too large to bridge.

Critiquing my mother's and sister's Witness activities was something I avoided doing. They did not talk much about Watchtower activities to me as that would be considered like *"casting their pearls before swine"* (Matthew 7: 6). I also wondered if they did not want to know anything about me for fear of discovering something that would force them to report me to the elders and then completely sever any remaining connection. Whatever their reasons, our interactions deteriorated to that of casual acquaintances. My heart ached, but I took what I could get. I loved my mother, sister, nephew and niece. I wanted my children to know and love their grandmother, aunt and cousins. Having lost one parent, I did not feel prepared to lose another. In spite of the deteriorating and superficial relationship, Terry purchased a townhouse for my mother. Mom invited a couple of pioneers to share the townhouse with her.

I cannot help but wonder if there had not been an ever-present threat and fear of being shunned by my family if I left the Witnesses, if I could have spared myself and my family all the prolonged agony of a slow fade out. It would have been so much easier to make a clean break from all the falsity and all the hypocrisy - if the immediate loss of my family had not been the punishment for so doing. Of course, such a complete break would really only have been possible if my husband and I had been on the same page at the same time – or so it seemed to me at the time. Again ... water under the bridge.

After a year or so, my sister and her husband (a brother she met while he was serving at the Toronto Bethel) sold their house in Ottawa and moved across the country to his hometown of Vancouver. For my mother it must have felt as if both her daughters had now been wrenched away from her. She consoled herself by redoubling her efforts in service to the Watchtower organization.

After a couple of years of not attending meetings, Terry and I decided that it was unfair to keeping adhering to some of the Witness practices, such as not celebrating birthdays, thanksgiving or Christmas, simply out of habit. Why should our children not enjoy the same activities as all their friends? It was time to totally embrace freedom for ourselves, and especially for our children, and do exactly as we pleased. It would also be easier to do these things without my sister, brother-in-law, nephew and niece living in the region.

The only time I had ever come close to 'celebrating' Christmas was when my parents, sister and I visited my father's step-sister, Jean and her husband. (Jean was the one who suffered terrible burns as a child while jumping over a candlestick.) She knew that as Jehovah's Witnesses we did not celebrate Christmas and decided she would place presents under their Christmas tree for each one of us. It was so unexpected and exciting to be handed gifts with your name on them, and open them to find items selected just for you. I recall being concerned that I should not express too much delight in front of my parents, at celebrating this 'bad' holiday, but when I peeked over at them they were grinning from ear to ear watching me open the gifts. Christmas, it seemed to my young self, was not 'bad' as I had been led to believe, but was a wonder-full, cozy, warm, family time.

I have to admit once Terry and I decided to join in all these *"worldly"* celebrations, I went a little over the top. It is *"more blessed to give than to receive"* and let me tell you it is a lot of fun! I had a blast preparing, decorating, and cooking for different holidays. I loved choosing, wrapping and giving gifts at my children's birthdays and at Christmas. Terry said I enjoyed it almost more than the children did. Well there was a child in me who was making up for many years of denial, loneliness and longing.

I remember dreary December days of my childhood, alone in our colorless JW world, while the world outside glistened with lights and rang out with joyful music. Everyone, it seemed, was participating in the festivities except us. I didn't care about missing out on the gifts, it was the warmth, the connections, the get-togethers, and the merriment of the festivities I wanted to enjoy.

Often as a young teen, to fill some of the empty hours around the Christmas holidays, JW friends would take us in their car at night to drive up and down the exclusive streets of "the Kingsway". The mansions there had the most exquisite Christmas decorations and apparently these Witness friends did not want us to miss out on viewing them. So there we were, a car crammed full of Jehovah's Witnesses driving around admiring the lights and decor of a holiday in which we could not participate. I'm sure they meant well, but it was a rather absurd gesture that even a kid such as myself could see as ironic. It just accentuated how excluded and separate we were ... and always would be. It must be said, however, that they made sure not to have Christmas carols playing on the radio during the Christmas lights tours!

Any worldly celebration that Terry and our family then embraced as ex-JWs, was done in a purely secular fashion. We had no interest in celebrating the birth of a baby Jesus. We used these times as opportunities to gather as a family - to invite friends - to celebrate our connections. These yearly celebrations became family get-together rituals that our children and now our grandchildren treasure. They have produced so many happy family memories. Our celebrations of them had nothing to do with religion and did not incite us to join any religion.

Family rituals are another thing that Jehovah's Witnesses are denied by not being able to join in common festivities and by being kept so busy they hardly have any time to develop any long-standing celebratory events for their families. And please, if you are a JW, don't try to tell me that circuit and district assemblies were our rituals! My husband was kept so busy working to keep those assemblies going that my children and I never saw him. Conventions forever seemed to gobble up our vacations and separate our family. They hurt rather than helped our family togetherness.

Once we had decided that we could no longer deny our children the right to enjoy the celebrations that took place in our community, we had to start from scratch. I began to prepare with some trepidation. Even shopping for Christmas gifts or Christmas wrapping paper had me looking over my shoulder anticipating the critical, ready-to-report eyes of members of our former congregation. Old JW beliefs and accompanying fears die hard. It was fascinating, in a macabre sort of way, to see how many of the JW patterns I had totally internalized. Because of being terrified of being disfellowshipped and losing contact with our family, we bent over backwards to keep our 'sinful' celebrations a secret. What a pitiful scenario on every level. We were out but we were not yet free of their insidious insinuations into our lives.

Dance, when you're broken open.
Dance, if you've torn the bandage off.
Dance, in the middle of fighting.
Dance, in your blood.
Dance, when you're perfectly free.
~Rumi

CHAPTER 36

'Corporate' Espionage

The autumn before our first Christmas I enrolled in Psychology and Creative Writing classes in the Continuing Education Department of a local college. I was also serving on the board of directors of a Fine Arts Center for children. As well, I had developed and led workshops for women wanting to set new personal and professional goals for themselves. (These workshops were based on the books of author/coach/therapist Barbara Sher.) The girl who felt she never got to do a thing she really wanted to do, was now finally busy doing many things she would never have been able to do as a JW - including preparing for her family's first Christmas - and she was loving it.

With all these activities afoot, I decided to get some outside help with the housework. Home cleaning businesses offering maid services were popular at the time. These companies would send in teams of four or five housecleaners who go through the house, cleaning from top to bottom, in an hour or two. Sounded good to me and I signed a contract with one of them.

We were often out when the cleaning team came to do their work. If we were at home we did our best to stay out of their way. We reasoned that the less interference they had from us, the quicker they could do their job, leave and not interrupt our family life. The workers were generally cheerful and friendly, but I really only had conversations with the team leader. Workers and I greeted each other with a quick "*hello*", but did not get into any lengthy conversations. They were there to do their job and leave as quickly as possible.

It never occurred to me to wonder who might be on the team sent to our home by the cleaning company - who would enter and roam around every room in our house so freely – who would dust our bookshelves and desktops – who would vacuum the floors of our closets and tidy trinkets and books on our coffee tables – who would see the notepad beside the kitchen telephone. You'd think that I might have connected the fact that denied an education many JWs are forced to take low-paying jobs in the service industry, with this new arrangement I had for a team of maids to clean my house? You get where I'm going with this, right?

Yes, you've got it. It seems that a JW woman, actually a former friend of mine from the local congregation, was on the team of house maids assigned to clean our house. She had a daughter the same age as our oldest daughter and she, Anna (not her real name) and her daughter had been guests in our home. She knew exactly where she was. She definitely knew she was cleaning Terry and Bonnie's home.

This sister, Anna, was not stupid. She must have known that it was just a tad unethical to be slinking around our house, trying to hide her presence while doing her job. She would have had to make sure she turned her back if I walked in a room, or rushed to bend over the bathtub or toilet if I walked past a bathroom when she was cleaning. She had to realize that if I discovered her roaming around my home I would have called the company and asked for them to remove her from the team. Of course, she realized it - that's why she must have made a point of hiding behind doors, drapes, furniture, whatever, as she did her work. No one in our family ever bumped into her (so she must have regularly hid herself) when the team was in our house.

If Anna had any sense of what was upright, ethical, and even Christian, she would have approached her boss and explained that cleaning our house was a conflict of interest for her. But then again, perhaps she realized that she had a unique opportunity no one else would ever have. She fell upon an opportunity to spy and report back to the elders about anything she could find in our home. Perhaps she considered it a unique opportunity to engage in *"theocratic warfare"* as a covert operative. I can imagine that it made her monotonous days cleaning people's homes a little more exciting.

I wondered exactly how far she went with her snooping? Did she open the drawers of our bedside tables? Did she put her hands in the pockets of coats and jackets hanging in our closets? Did she peek in our medicine cabinets? Did she examine the books on our bookshelves? Did she read the notes beside our telephones? Did she snoop amongst our children's belongings? Did she take note of the type of music we listened to and the films we watched? Did she take notes or photos while in our house? Just how far did her stealth violations of our privacy go?

The only thing that finally alerted us to the unethical presence of JW Anna in our house was a letter from the elders of our former congregation (and Anna's current congregation) demanding that we present ourselves before a judicial committee. Apparently someone had made a report to them that there were Christmas preparations going on in our home. This ghastly offense required the immediate convening of a kangaroo court! They must have been happy to finally have an accusation that could help them publicly denounce and evict us from the congregation.

It took us a while to figure out who could possibly have made such a report. Was somebody sneaking around outside our house and looking through our windows? Were our decorations visible through our front windows? Finally, I had an intuition and asked the house cleaning company owner for the names of the people on the cleaning team. Of course! One of the names was JW Anna. I felt the rage of someone who had been violated … probably because we had had our home penetrated by someone there for a purpose other than the one they disclosed! I was disgusted and furious.

I made my own report to the owner of the house cleaning company about the 'corporate espionage' that had transpired in our home. One of the employees of *her organization* was spying on us and conveying the information to *another organization*. The owner was shocked that one of her employees would be making secret reports to some other organization about what was going on in the privacy of a client's house. Justifiably concerned about her legal liability, the owner told me JW Anna would be fired. By the way, JW Anna was the daughter of "*Sister Anointed*" whom you may have read about in my book "*Exiting the JW Cult: A Healing Handbook*". Seems that that JW family was really out to accuse, incriminate, and shame us in any way they could. What else would good Christians and former friends want to do?

My husband wrote a terse letter in response to the elders' letter, saying that we felt no need to submit to their demand to appear before their kangaroo court, aka judicial committee, and would not now or ever accede to their delusions of power over our public or private behaviors. He told them that what went on in the privacy of our home was nobody's business - according to the most basic laws of moral decency. He reminded them that since they were the willing recipients of information collected under unethical, false pretenses by a member of their group, about our private affairs, we were in a position to take legal action against them. If they continued their efforts to publicly denounce us for what went on in the privacy of our home, we would take legal action against their 'corporate' spy, themselves, and the organization they represented.

One elder came to our door and tried in person to persuade Terry to appear before the committee. Terry calmly, politely but firmly repeated in person what he had already said in the letter. It was a weird encounter as this was a brother younger than Terry who had looked up to and modeled himself on Terry (as a young pioneer and novice elder) for years.

As far as we know, we were not disfellowshipped. Perhaps they felt they could not proceed because of our threat of legal action and because of the *"two witness rule"*. They only had informant Anna's account of the 'terrible, heathen, unholy Christmas scene' she found in our home. If it was ever announced from the platform that we were no longer a part of the organization or should be shunned, we were not informed of it. It seemed the Witnesses would have to keep spying on us to find a credible disfellowshipping offense – and, of course, have two witnesses to any offense. They never did find anything with which they could accuse us - but the spying continued in one form or another. The ever-present threat of being formally cast out and totally shunned loomed like a 'death' sentence from which there was no escape or appeal.

"Absolute faith corrupts as absolutely as absolute power." ~Eric Hoffer

The elders from our old circuit had the difficult task of trying to explain how a well-respected and much loved elder, Terry (and his problem wife) could slip away from *'the truth'*. It would have made their task much easier if they could have demonstrated that we were participating in activities considered unbiblical, pagan and/or demonic by the cult. An example of further spying and intrusion was when our daughter, told us that a Jehovah's Witness schoolmate informed her that she was going to tell the brothers at the Kingdom Hall that Taira had been seen giving a birthday present to a classmate. It infuriated me that JW children were also spying on our children at school and reporting them to these jurist wannabes, as if they could ever have any authority over our lives! That was what was so crazy-making. They didn't ... yet they did.

Yes, we had left and now possessed a happiness and contentment with how our lives were unfolding that we had never known as JWs. And still ... the Watchtower continued to try to reach into our lives interfering with our choices and our right to privacy. Leaving the Watchtower is like trying to leave the mafia. It is almost certain you will be persona non grata, be stalked, be shunned, and certainly be menaced with the threat of death at the ultimate turf war of Armageddon. On top of that, and even more insidious, much of the Watchtower's programming still lurks between our own ears affecting our thoughts, emotions and behaviour for a good while after exiting.

> "I am grateful to those who have betrayed me... They thought they were just stabbing me in the back, but they were also cutting me free from their poisonous life." ~Steven Maraboli

The Watchtower Bible & Tract Society has an undeniable record of interfering in the lives of families and that violates Article 12 of the Universal Declaration of Human Rights, which says: "*No one shall be subjected to arbitrary interference with his privacy, family, home or correspondence, not to attacks upon his honour and reputation. Everyone has the right to the protection of the law against such interference or attacks.*" The Universal Declaration of Human Rights was adopted by the United Nations after the Second World War on December 10, 1948 and has been translated into more than 350 languages worldwide. The WBTS has been in clear violation during all the years of the existence of these universally declared human rights. This religion-cum-corporate-cult must be held to account for its interference in millions of lives of private citizens and families - interference under the guise of ushering them through their lies about "*the end of the world*" and their fantasy reward of "*eternal life on a paradise earth.*"

Terry in dark suit (second from right) and me (third from right) with our children, Terry's parents, Terry's brother and sister-in-law and their children, outside of a Kingdom Hall in Brantford, Ontario, Canada. We were now inactive JWs, but attended the wedding of a JW relative with our family. This photograph was taken just before our experience with Watchtower 'corporate' espionage.

"Sorrow prepares you for joy. It violently sweeps everything out of your house, so that new joy can find space to enter. It shakes the yellow leaves from the bough of your heart, so that fresh, green leaves can grow in their place. It pulls up the rotten roots, so that new roots hidden beneath have room to grow." ~Rumi

CHAPTER 37

Life – OUT

Once *out* and being shunned by so-called friends in the congregation, I felt as if I had been set adrift, having no map of the new territory and no clue as to a destination. There was nowhere to go, no one to call, and I felt profoundly alone, unsure - even desolate. A couple of times I hoped a little shopping trip and a nice lunch at one of my favorite restaurants would cheer me up. I wandered like a zombie through the aisles of shops unable to focus or care about any of the beautiful things on display. At lunch I sat alone and tried to eat while tears streamed down my cheeks. I felt unmoored, confused, bereft and profoundly alone.

In the midst of this disorientation and grief, I had little inner access to constructive or creative ideas for my life. Try as I might, I could not imagine a future – apart from loving and raising my children. With time, and after a lot of tears, the despair and paralysis began to subside. Finally there seemed to be more energy available to imagine and create a new life. We enrolled our children in activities at a fine arts centre where they learned to play musical instruments and took courses in ballet, drama and/or gymnastics. There were other parents there with whom I struck up friendships. Adult education courses at the local college provided intellectual stimulation and opportunities to meet like-minded people. Now *out* we had free time to enjoy activities with our children, some as simple as hiking, apple-picking, outdoor sports such as cross-country skiing, and our favorite - evenings at home with the children, playing classical or pop music while freely dancing, exercising and laughing together in the basement playroom.

Now *out* and having reclaimed Sundays for ourselves, we lingered over breakfasts enjoying conversing with our children and spent Sunday afternoons on excursions to the library, engaging in sports, or laughing ourselves silly playing board-games. Time reclaimed from the incessant, life-consuming demands of the Watchtower went into good times with our children and solidifying family bonds. I could not allow myself to wallow in any more self-pity, regret or bitterness because of the losses due to leaving the JW organization.

The best evidence of having made the right decision for ourselves and our family would be to create a good, fulfilling life. Our children were thriving, as was Terry's new business, and I experienced a surge in creativity. I wrote a manuscript for a book entitled, "*The Pregnancy Primer & Journal*". Having no luck pitching it to publishers I tried, unsuccessfully, to adapt it into a newsletter. A few years later, an uncannily similar and successful book appeared on bestseller lists entitled "*What to Expect When You're Expecting*". It is now in its 4th edition and has made millions. My timing and marketing skills missed the boat on that one. Close, but no cigar. Next I wrote a little book for parents and children entitled "*The Latchkey Children's Ledger*". Annik Press, publisher of children's books, accepted the book for publication. I was over the moon and could not believe my luck! Unfortunately, a few weeks after accepting the book they informed me that they had "*regretfully changed their mind*". Bummer! Close, but no cigar – again. After some self-initiated study on the topic of creativity and problem-solving, I developed a personal problem-solving game I called "*Mind Moves*". One weekend I set out, uninvited, to an International Toy Fair being held in Toronto. I walked around with my prototype of the game in a big shopping bag, and the first game manufacturer to whom I shyly pitched it, decided to keep it for further evaluation! Whoa! Was my luck about to change? The company assessing "*Mind Moves*" was the company that produced the wildly popular game "*Trivial Pursuit*" - Chieftan Products (*Trivial Pursuit* is now owned by Hasbro). In a letter received two months later they said they had spent weeks testing *Mind Moves*, but had regretfully decided it was "*too up-market*" for the general population. They suggested I try to "*adapt it into a tool for corporate training*". (Eventually I used portions of *Mind Moves* in a course I taught on *Creative Thinking & Problem-Solving* at the college level.) Close again, but still … no cigar. Perhaps life knew, that being an ex-JW, I was not prepared to smoke!

In spite of those disappointments, life was busy, rewarding and good. There were occasional moments when I would fall back into sadness or despair (because of the superficial relationship with my mother and sister) but I was able to remind myself that progress usually consists of two steps forward and one step back. It seemed there was no choice but to trust the process of life – the good, the bad, the disheartening and the everyday. We had each other and we had our lives back. That was, ultimately, all we needed. That, in fact, was huge.

While doing therapy as one of the components of my Gestalt therapy training, the therapist, a forthright German holocaust survivor named Susan Saros (who had lost many members of her family of origin in the concentration camps), asked if I had ever conducted a search for my father. As the answer "*No*" left my lips, I immediately felt embarrassed. When she asked, "*Why not?*" I was puzzled by my seeming lack of curiosity and lack of initiative. She shared that if she had any hope a parent was still alive, she would move heaven and earth to find them. We discussed the implications of conducting a search for my father and none of them seemed too intimidating – except for the first face to face encounter.

With Susan's encouragement, I moved past my JW learned helplessness and decided to try to find my father. He would then have been eligible for Canada's pension plan payment to seniors – assuming he was still a resident of Canada, so I wrote to the Canadian government department overseeing pension payments, asking if they could reveal the address of one Irvine MacEwan to his daughter. A letter arrived saying that due to the Privacy Act of Canada, they could not give any pertinent details concerning my request. *However*, as a onetime compassionate act, they would be willing to take a letter from me and mail it to him. That would protect his privacy and give him the choice as to whether he wanted to renew contact or not. Wow!

Of course, there could be some very interesting things that could come to light as a result of this initiative. Had my father remarried? He was only in his early forties when he disappeared, so it was highly probable. Did I now have half-brothers and half-sisters? How would a new family feel about contact with his old family? Could he be ill, alone and/or needing care? So many unknowns. But I decided to proceed anyway and invited my sister in Vancouver to prepare her own letter that would be included in the package. We wrote letters, telling him about our lives and our children. We included photographs of our families. I told him that I was no longer one of Jehovah's Witnesses, hoping that might make him feel more comfortable about renewing contact. We sent off a package full of hope, forgiveness and photographs to the Canadian Pension Department which would then forward it to him. Then we waited ... and waited ... and waited ...

Finally after weeks of waiting, my sister and I had to admit there would be no reply to the missive from his deserted children. He either did not want to reunite with us or could not. Perhaps our letters were intercepted by a new spouse or a child that did not want their family disturbed by his original family. Perhaps he never even read our letters or saw the photographs of his grandchildren. It felt like another gut-wrenching rejection. My sister and I had to somehow come to terms with the disappointment. What choice did we have?

As mentioned, I made my way to university and acquired a few degrees and diplomas. I also took training programs outside the university setting, in different schools of psychotherapy. Had I remained a Jehovah's Witness I would not have enjoyed the privilege of walking the halls of academia and learning from so many talented people. One of my professors invited me to become her teaching assistant. She was generous with her time and encouragement and included me in the planning and teaching of each class on "*Interpersonal & Group Dynamics*". This professor, Mary Scott, took me under her wing and became a mentor – but even more, she became a treasured friend. Mary was not only a professor but also a psychological counsellor at the university For all intents and purposes I had lost my mother and sister, but with Mary Scott I found a sister of the heart.

Jack Shonkoff, MD, director of the Center on the Developing Child and professor at Harvard University says that compassionate mentors can help remediate toxic stress and help attenuate years of adverse childhood experiences (*Childhood Disrupted*, 2015, Jackson Nakazawa). Often the unplanned "*remediation*" for the stress and adversity happens because the mentor/friend provides a safe "*corrective emotional experience*" (one that was not available to us as children). Had I remained a JW I would never have found such an affirming friend and mentor. Mary mirrored my competencies and encouraged me to move on to pursue a master's degree.

Once licensed as a psychotherapist, I had the privilege of hearing the stories of hundreds of people and helping them make sense of their lives, come to terms with the particular realities of their existence, and learn how to support and love themselves throughout the whole exciting process of this sometimes crazy thing we call life. Education continued after obtaining a Master's Degree by taking training programs in *Psychotraumatology*, *Eye Movement Desensitization & Reprocessing* (EMDR) *therapy*, *drama therapy*, and more. Throughout, I had the privilege of meeting amazing people – professors, students, trainers and clients alike!

Clearly I was extremely fortunate to be able to undertake these study programs. I know not everyone can do so in mid-life when there are so many demands on time, energy and financial resources. It helped to have a supportive husband who provided a comfortable living for our family, and who encouraged all my endeavours. I recognize that I was advantaged, and have done my best to use those advantages to benefit others.

While acquiring an education, a profession and new friends was deeply satisfying, it did not compensate for the lack of an authentic and meaningful relationship with my mother and my sister. I spent a long time mourning their loss but eventually came to terms with the choices they made to obey the edicts of the Watchtower. They were under the influence of JW mind-control techniques and coerced by threats of banishment and destruction which pushed them to treat me as a casual acquaintance, and since my mother's death, for my sister to cut me off completely. They had such a large investment of time, energy and self in JW.ORG and could never entertain the idea of leaving this central organizing factor in their lives.

In spite of not having the enjoyment and comfort of close family ties, in spite of our children not having any aunts, uncles or cousins who valued them, Terry and I created and nurtured one beautiful, little family. Due to what I now recognize as generalized anxiety after all the stress of being raised as a Jehovah's Witness, I was probably a rather over-protective mother of my young children. My studies in the field of psychology, however, helped me become a better mother than I ever could have been straight out of the cult. It's a joy to observe my only child with children strike a beautiful balance as a parent, between what the father of child psychiatry, D.W. Winnicott called *"non-interference and non-abandonment"* of her children. Her amazing parenting skills reassure me that I was at least what Winnicott calls *"the good-enough mother"*.

Our three children have become fine, decent, upstanding people without the input of the Watchtower organization. (It's just amazing that our children did not become drug addicts and/or criminals because of not being raised *"in the truth"*, as we were warned would be the case!) I have so much respect and admiration for each one of these human beings we call our children. I often wonder if we would have remained so close to them if we have been trying to force them to live according to the edicts of the Watchtower. Frankly I doubt it. Each of our children has made a point to thank Terry and I for fading out of the JW cult. They know their lives are the better and the richer for it.

Once out of the organization I was busy with family, home, creative projects, education, career and a social life. I wanted nothing to do with the Watchtower or its Witnesses, did not know any ex-Witnesses apart from my husband, and just quietly went about my life. It was always a little weird having to explain to friends why we had no contact with family – why the children had no cousins – why there was never any extended family involved in our Thanksgivings or Christmases. We simply concentrated on our family unit and with time developed friends with whom we had close ties.

Years later I watched a couple of television documentaries exposing misdeeds among the Jehovah's Witnesses. The revelations piqued my interest and after a Google search, I became aware that there was an ex-JW community, but I had no idea of the extent to which this ex-JW community was active and growing. Since, as a psychotherapist, I did not want to be on Facebook or any other platform that risks compromising the client/therapist relationship, I did not know about the ex-JW support groups available on Facebook. Only once semi-retired did I finally create a Facebook page using a pseudonym, (still to protect therapeutic relationships from too much familiarity). But, I'm jumping ahead in my story once again.

CHAPTER 38

You're Kidding ... Right?

You could tell it was her first time. She looked around furtively as she entered the consultation room, her body language indicating that she was considering bolting back out the door. I smiled and gestured in the direction of a chair and took mine.

Me: Is this your first time visiting a therapist? I asked.
Client: Yes.
Me: It's normal to be a little nervous on your first visit. The unknown is always a bit scary, but all you have to do is talk truthfully about yourself and the situation that brings you here. So, (looking in my empty file) I notice that I don't have a referral here ... who referred you to me?
Client: I don't have a referral, I just did a search for "psychotherapist" and decided I would take the name at the bottom of the list.
Me: And you arrived at the letter "Z". Let me tell you a bit about how we will proceed. You will do most of the talking. I will listen and occasionally take notes of what you say. You are welcome to view the notes at any time. Everything discussed here is confidential. The only exception to that rule is that I am required by law to report to the authorities any information that indicates you or someone else could be harmed. Do you understand?
Client: Yes.
Me: So ... why don't you begin by telling me a little bit about yourself and the situation that brings you here.

She remained silent for several seconds.
Client: *I don't know where or how to begin - it's so - complicated.* More silence . . . . *I'm just not sure if I can explain things well enough so that you will understand.*
Me: *It's my job to find a way to understand. You just have to worry about telling me about yourself.*
Client: *Well ... I belong to a religion that is a bit strange ... A religion that has so many rules, so many requirements for everything. It even has its own terms for things. I don't know ... it will be hard to explain it all to you.*
Me: *Just try ... if there is something I don't understand, I will ask for more details.*
Client: *Well, I'm one of Jehovah's Witnesses. I haven't talked to anyone in the religion about my situation or my feelings because they would probably pass on what I say to the elders of the congregation and I don't want that.*

She proceeded to tentatively outline her situation. I could sense she still had little hope I could ever really understand her predicament. She had not settled back into her chair and she wrung her hands as she spoke. After a few minutes, as she paused I took the opportunity to speak.
Me: *Well I guess it is really fortuitous that you made your selection from the bottom of the list of therapists that came up in your search.*

She raised her head to look at me and wrinkled her forehead into a kind of question.
Me: *Your strategy of choosing the last therapist on the list, led you to pick the only former Jehovah's Witness psychotherapist in this area. I was raised as a Jehovah's Witness and left the sect over twenty years ago.*

Her eyes widened into saucers and her mouth fell open.
Me: *My great grandfather, my grandmother and my mother were Witnesses. Every relative I have, except for my father, is a Witness. I was a pioneer, a special pioneer, married to an elder, and if not for a surprise pregnancy would have ended up with my husband in circuit work. So your concerns about my not being able to understand can be put to rest.*

She slowly shook her head back and forth in what I took to be a kind of amazement.
Client: *You're kidding ... right?*
Me: *I wouldn't do that.*

Her eyes filled with tears. She cried - clearly with relief. She had made a really serendipitous selection of psychotherapist. We were both amazed at the synchronicity of it all.

The actual therapy with this client must, of course, remain confidential. The exchange above is my best approximation of the specifics-free, opening exchange between us. Nothing shared above violates the unidentified client's privacy. You actually learn more about me than her. It was just such an unusual way, for someone seeking a therapist for the first time, to find one who had not only the therapeutic skills they needed but the personal experience of having been a member of the same high-control group. Twenty years plus, after leaving the Jehovah's Witnesses and finally getting an education it was a privilege to be able to help this woman dealing with similar issues to the ones I had dealt with so many years before. I still marvel at the synchronicity that led her to find a therapist who had 'been there, done that'.

Unfortunately, few Jehovah's Witnesses or ex-JWs will find a therapist who has spent any time in a cult. Therapists cannot possibly have had every experience that every client has had. But most therapists understand the dynamics and effects of abuse, of trauma, of loss, of grief, of isolation and loneliness and should be able to help you with yours, whatever the origins. You will have to explain your unique cult experience and then the two of you will work together in a therapeutic relationship on the road to your recovery. (One ex-JW has reported back to me that she shared my book *"Exiting the JW Cult: A Healing Handbook"* with her therapist and that it helped the therapist better understand what she, the client, had experienced in the cult.) Trust the process. It usually works.

While helping people from a variety of backgrounds was always a privilege, I was especially honored to be able to offer my therapeutic skill set to that Jehovah's Witness client. Of course as a therapist it is not my place to tell any client how to live their life. A good therapist facilitates the client's process in finding their own answers to the questions life presents them. While the ex-JW in me might have wanted to scream, *"Get out of that cult, ASAP!"* my job was to help her formulate her own conclusions about her one and only life. Good therapists are not advice-giving, shame-inducing, ratings-conscious television therapists. It is inappropriate and invasive for a therapist to impose their answers on a client's life.

Our work together was largely spent re-building self-esteem, re-establishing the ability to think critically and build self-trust, enough so that she could act on her own understanding of life. She left therapy equipped to stand up for herself and empowered to live her life in her own way. I do not know the end of her story. My hope is that the insights gained in this course of therapy were used to enhance her one and only life.

CHAPTER 39

Hey Mom ... Over Here

After my sister and her family moved to Vancouver, my mother continued to live on her own in Ottawa. We visited her every couple of months and she occasionally came to Montreal to visit us. For example, she came and stayed with us after the births of our last two babies and she was a great help and a loving grandmother. Eventually she stopped visiting, perhaps due to having less energy for travel as she aged. She would sometimes receive us in her home and talk with me by phone.

During her last few years living in Ottawa, my mother was 'privileged', as they say, to appear in some of the Bible dramas put on at the District (Regional) Conventions. She considered this to be a high honor and a recognition of her years of service in the Watchtower organization. I'm happy she had such acknowledgments. We even went to one convention to see her play the role of Naomi in one of these much-hyped Bible dramas.

Due to health concerns it was becoming clear that Mom should no longer live alone. She gave not a moment's thought of coming to live with us, however. Mom could never reside with anyone, even her eldest daughter and her family, who had made the choice to leave the JW organization. It was hurtful that our family and home were not worthy of consideration, but at the same time it would have been a huge challenge to raise our children with her religious fervor and judgmental JW eye scanning our every move. So ultimately we were okay with her moving to live with her only believing daughter in Vancouver.

Knowing that this would be a huge task and adjustment for her, we did all we could to facilitate her move. I helped her sort through her possessions and make the hard decisions about what she would take and what she would leave behind. Terry had heavy pieces of her belongings professionally packed, and paid for shipping all the boxes the three thousand miles to Vancouver. We were happy to help and tried to keep the sorting and letting go process light and easy for her.

As her departure date came closer, I assured her that I would drive from Montreal to Ottawa, take her to the airport and see her off. Vanessa (13) and Jordan (12) came along to say farewell to their grandmother. I knew she could have easily asked one of her JW friends to drive her to the airport, so I was touched that she wanted her actual family to do it.

Once packed up in the car, and on the way to the airport, Mom told us about one of the going-away parties the brothers in Ottawa had had for her the night before. Apparently a lot of kind things were said and she was leaving feeling that her presence had been much appreciated in the Ottawa JW community. Then she casually mentioned that a couple of her Bible studies and a couple of sisters would also be coming to the airport to say goodbye. I said, "*Oh, they weren't able to go to the goodbye party last night?*" She replied, "*Oh they were at the party but they want to see me off today, too.*" I had not expected there to be a group of JWs with us at the airport, but it seemed I had no choice in the matter. I should have anticipated as much.

Once at the airport, Mom spotted her Witness friends and waved enthusiastically. After introductions, I realized that I knew one of the sisters - a lovely young woman who had actually lived in my mother's townhouse while she pioneered in Ottawa.

Mom's JW friends clustered around her. One of them already had tears in her eyes. Mom could only direct her attention in so many directions, and it seemed that she needed to bask in the affection and adoration coming her way from her Bible students and JW friends. Vanessa, Jordan and I hung out on the periphery while they chatted and hugged. Mom's friends did not interact with my children or myself after the introductions had been made. I guess they knew about Mom's daughter's "*inactive*" status. I was not sure if they were preoccupied with saying goodbye to my mother or if they were purposely shunning us – nor did I care. I just wanted to spend these last few moments together as grandmother, mother and grandchildren.

Finally we all wandered over to where there were tables and chairs so that Mom could sit down. I offered to get some coffee or tea for everybody and took their orders. Mom and her JW friends sat around two tables that had been pushed together for a large group.

Vanessa and Jordan sat on some upholstered benches at a distance from the group at the tables, while I went to get the drinks. I came back to the tables with the cups of tea and coffee and distributed them around to everyone making sure anyone who wanted cream or sugar got them. There seemed to be no room for more chairs around the two tables and so, for a while, I just stood behind my mother. Mom was busy chatting away with her friends and she didn't think to try and squeeze her daughter and grandchildren into the group. Finally I moved back over to where my children were seated, not wanting them to feel totally left out and forgotten.

Sitting at a distance from the group with my children, I looked over at my mother soaking up the attention from her JW sisters *"in the truth"* and her Bible study protégés. It struck me what a perfect picture this was of where my mother's allegiances lay. She had cast her lot with all things Watchtower and was willing to leave her unbelieving blood relatives on the periphery of her attention ... and her life. It had never been so clear. The C.S. Day-Lewis poem below describes how I felt in this scene at the Ottawa airport:

> *I have had worse partings, but none that so*
> *Gnaws at my mind still. Perhaps it is roughly*
> *Saying what God alone could perfectly show -*
> *How selfhood begins with a walking away,*
> *And love is proved in the letting go.*
> ~C. Day-Lewis
> Walking Away

(Only when editing this book did I notice that I had inserted this same piece of C. S. Lewis poetry after a parting with my father (Chapter 20), and now in reference to a parting with my mother. I am leaving it that way, because Lewis' words so beautifully express the gnawing hurt and the existential necessity of not collapsing because of the pain of the partings with each of my parents – both partings being strongly influenced by our association with the Watchtower organization.)

Despite all my seeming adult understanding and insights, the needy, abandoned child in me felt profoundly rejected and hurt by being excluded from my mother's side just before her departure. Directly before me was an image in real time of my mother, albeit unconsciously, viewing myself and my family as basically dead to her, as she was expected to do by the Watchtower. I don't think she had even noticed that she had not included us in the group spending the last minutes with her before her departure. Jordan, Vanessa and I were excluded from the group for a significant chunk of time. Clearly Mom wanted to spend her last few minutes with her JW family not her DNA family.

The kind sister that had lived with my mother noticed that my children and myself had been excluded from the group and got up and tried to place two chairs beside her now empty chair. She motioned to us to come over, sit down and join the group. I felt too depleted emotionally to do anything but acquiesce. This kind sister met my eyes, and though nothing was said, conveyed that she had picked up on the hurtful dynamic. So we got to sit near Mom, in the group, for a few minutes. We were not, however, included in the conversation.

Mom's flight was announced and she had to say her goodbyes. Her groupies seemed to finally have the sensitivity to allow the family members alone be the ones who walked her to the boarding gate. Our goodbyes and hugs with Mom were tight and the four of us had tears flowing. We watched her walk away to board the airplane, waved and began to make our way back to the parking area. My emotions were raw, but I gathered all the strength I had to push them down until we got back to the car. Thank goodness the JW groupies were gone and we did not have to deal with encountering them again.

Back in the car, all the emotions I'd been suppressing for the last couple of hours spilled out. I began to weep. My kids thought I was crying about Mom moving so far away, and of course that was a big part of it. The deepest emotion however, was really about seeing so clearly where my family and I stood with regard to my mother's affections and priorities.

I tell this story as an example of how regular JWs, due to their indoctrination, can so easily cut off loved ones who have left the cult. I don't think my mother consciously made a decision that she would exclude us at the airport, but it was evident that her mind and heart were with her JW cohorts and not with her *"inactive"* daughter and grandchildren. She did not totally shun us from her life because of my fading away, but she did exclude us from her circle at an important moment, foreshadowing more rigid treatment and exclusion to come.

Mom lived with my JW sister and her family in Vancouver for 16 years. When one of my children and I travelled the three thousand miles to see them we were warmly greeted – perhaps because I was not yet officially disfellowshipped. It was surprising to see that they even skipped service and the meetings on Sundays to take us to view tourist landmarks such as Whistler Mountain. It was fun to be together, even though we all tiptoed around the topic of religion and what my daughter and I were doing with our *"heathen"* lives.

Four generations from left to right, my daughter Taira, Taira's daughter Indya, my Mother, me and my Sister. This photo was taken when I was completely inactive and my daughter Taira and I brought my Mother's first great-granddaughter to meet her. Now Mom is dead and my sister, due to 'new light', totally shuns me and my family.

Once my mother died in 2009, communication from my sister dwindled to a bare minimum. It occurred to me that part of her warm welcomes to our previous visits must have been in deference to allowing my mother to keep some sort of relationship with her other daughter and grandchildren. I emailed my sister a couple of years ago to tell her I missed her and to ask for news of her and her family. She did the courtesy of sending a brief email in reply. I was shocked to hear that my niece had one child that was given the same name as my son (as if my son did not exist), and that my niece had recently had a second baby. My sister had not bothered to let me know. But she had let me know with that lack of reaching out, that lack of inclusion, how peripheral I was in her life. She didn't even inquire into the health status of our daughter who had had major cancer surgery a couple of years previous. I just did not recognize the remote, insensitive person she seemed to have become in order to obey the governing body's requirement to shun me. So deeply hurtful. So absolutely unnecessary. All due to edicts of old, out-of-touch men at the top of a corporate cult in New York.

That email stung and held a lot of implicit information about how my sister was now required to, and would, view our relationship. I have since become aware that due to all the defections from the ranks of the JWs, the governing body is becoming ever more rigid about associating with anyone who has left the fold - to the point of telling members to not even exchange emails with them. "*Really, what your beloved family member needs to see is your resolute stance to put Jehovah above everything else -- including the family bond ... Do not look for excuses to associate with a disfellowshipped family member, for example, through e-mail.*" (Watchtower, Jan 15, 2013, p. 16) Wow!

It horrifies me that my sister and her children are actually counseled by the Governing Body to hate me for my "*badness*" in turning away from the religion. Here is what was said in the July 15th, 1961 Watchtower: "*...God's Word also says to "hate what is bad". When a person persists in a way of badness after knowing what is right ... then **in order to hate what is bad a Christian must hate the person** with whom the badness is inseparably linked.*" To interfere and rupture family bonds with such cruel counsel is unconscionable! Orders to hate and then to expect that hate to be demonstrated by ostracizing family members, surely constitutes a hate crime.

"People wrap themselves in their beliefs. And they do it in such a way that you can't set them free. Not even the truth will set them free." ~Michael Specter

CHAPTER 40

Millions Now Loyal, Will Also Die

It almost seems as if, at her death, my mother's wacky sense of humor was still at work. Somehow, she managed to die on my birthday. What are the chances of that? So now, when my husband and children celebrate my birthday, I remember too, that it is the day of my mother's death. When I can, I smile and silently applaud Mom for her 'wicked' timing. Of course, it must be a coincidence ... but it tickles my fancy to imagine my mother somehow arranging to evermore insert herself and, thereby, her JW beliefs into all my 'heathen' birthday celebrations. Touché, Mom!

After being informed of my mother's death, at almost ninety-one years of age, there was a lot of agonizing about whether or not to travel the three thousand miles to her Jehovah's Witness funeral. In the end I decided not to attend. For one thing, having recently recovered from a bout of pneumonia I was not sure I had the physical strength to make the long trip to Vancouver. As well, I had often seen JW funerals used as a means to witness to non-believers or even condemn and chastise ex-members in attendance. I wanted the funeral to be wholly devoted to my mother who had given over seventy years of her life in service to them. It would have been terrible, in my view, if the funeral somehow became a vehicle to try and shepherd me or anyone else back into the fold. I wanted the funeral to be a gathering to honor my mother, and only that.

While discussing whether or not to go, I recall telling my husband that if in attendance at the funeral and the elder presiding started to direct exhortations my way, or tried to use the funeral as a vehicle to *give a witness*, I was not sure whether I would be able to restrain myself from jumping up and telling them to give my mother her due and leave their witnessing, and me, out of it! It was probably best for me to stay away from the proceedings and avoid creating any sort of scene that could upset my grieving sister. I sent a large wreath of flowers with a note attached containing private sentiments, and that would have to suffice. At our next family get-together the five of us sat and informally eulogized Mom, sharing endearing and amusing memories.

My sister informed us that we could dial-in by telephone and hear the funeral service in Vancouver. It was scheduled for Valentine's Day – February 14th. Apparently, one of my JW elder cousins would be delivering the opening prayer. My eldest daughter and I both dialed-in to listen.

As the funeral talk began, we heard my cousin invited to say the opening prayer. As he began, another male voice came over the telephone line saying he would need to have all the names of everyone remotely listening to the funeral. Gilead graduates, bethel members, special pioneers, long-time JWs from all over Canada who had dialed in to hear the funeral, all obediently, one by one, gave their name (and spelled it when necessary) to this brother - *during the prayer*! I was aghast and refused to interrupt and disrespect my mother's funeral by answering this brother's ill-timed question. My daughter followed suit and remained silent too.

Beyond being annoyed that I could not hear a word of my cousin's prayer while names were given, I could not believe that not one of these long-time, "*spiritually mature*" JWs had the where-with-all (guts) to say, "*Brother, could we give you our names after the prayer or better yet after the funeral talk?*" They were just non-thinking, dutiful clones who did what the elder asked them to do - even if it interrupted a prayer to their God, Jehovah. Now don't get me wrong, I did not want to hear the prayer because I wanted to pray to Jehovah. I just wanted to hear my cousin's words and be respectful of the entire funeral service. Instead, my daughter and I experienced another glaring example of the level of unthinking, rote obedience in operation in that organization.

The rest of the service was a fine testimony to my mother and I felt gratified that she was thus honored. After all, she had given her life in service of their goals. However, talking with my sister later, I wanted her to know that we had been listening to the entire service by phone, but I knew our names would not appear on that unthinking brother's phone list. I told her about the interruption on the phone line right in the middle of the prayer, and how only we two non-JWs respected the prayer instead of answering the ill-timed request. She perhaps heard too much disdain in my voice and was not particularly receptive to that report.

The following text is an excerpt from the pamphlet my sister prepared for my mother's funeral. My sister's devotion to our mother and to the JW organization and their belief system is evident throughout:

> And we take comfort in knowing that when Clara is resurrected to a paradise earth, her dreams of enjoying Jehovah's creations in peace and contentment with good health will finally be fulfilled.
>
> Clara's greatest love was reading, studying, meditating and sharing Jehovah's precious words of truth with others. On first moving to the 'big city' she didn't know anybody, so spent her time reading her Concordance along with her King James Bible, which explains her extensive knowledge of the scriptures!
>
> Her life was filled with adventure and love, sadness and heartache, but she did not dwell on what was lacking and so deeply enjoyed all the precious little basics of life, like a good piece of bread and butter and jam and a hot cup of tea. She was greatly respected and admired for her endurance under trials and faithfulness despite hardships and had a reputation as a tireless worker in the field service. Clara was loved for her honesty and fortitude and steadfastly raised her two girls alone in good humour, relying on Jehovah and the spiritual, moral and physical support of many dear brothers and sisters in the various congregations she attended throughout the many moves of her life.
>
> *The preceding comments are the kind words expressed by many who knew and loved her – including her daughters, Bonnie and Ann, grandchildren, nephews, nieces, cousins, her two sister's, Elizabeth and Marie, and many long time friends.*

My mother lived happy to be a Jehovah's Witness. I'm glad that she found some life satisfaction in her choice to labor for the Watchtower, although I know she suppressed many of her natural talents to be in their service. I hope she was not aware of all she missed as a result. At the end, however, Mom was suffering from dementia and thus was perhaps spared the knowledge and disappointment that she had invested her one and only life in an unforgivable lie and would not live to see the promised reward of everlasting life in paradise. Millions of other loyal Jehovah's Witnesses, like my mother, will also die – unrewarded for all their years of service.

I often wonder if Mom felt she had lost her husband because of her devotion to the Witnesses. I know it broke her heart to lose him. I also know that I further pained her precious heart when I left the Witnesses. I hate that my exit hurt her ... and yet I would still claim my one and only life, away from Watchtower interference, if I had to do it over again.

It was much harder for my sister when my mother died than it was for me. I had already been mourning the loss of my mother for years. The relationship between my Mother and I was never the same once I faded out of the Jehovah's Witnesses. I really lost her way back then and had grieved that loss ever since – especially after the airport scene. Then, with the death of our mother, I lost my sister, the only remaining member of my family of origin, to total shunning.

The loss of every member of my family of origin has been due, in some measure, to my former membership in the Watchtower Society and due to the Watchtower's unwelcome interference in my life. After all the time, all the personal work, and all the help I have had in order to come to terms with these losses, it still makes my heart ache to write about it here. I can only imagine how many more family ruptures and how much more heartache the Watchtower has caused to millions of people around the globe.

Their methods were especially crude and most of these former friends were now born again model citizens; lobotomized; or burnt out shells. ~ H.M. Forester

But listen to me.
For one moment
Quit being sad.
Hear blessings
Dropping their blossoms
Around you.
~ Rumi

Epilogue

As said, after the death of my mother, there was an abrupt end to the already minimal relationship I had with my only sister. The instructions of the governing body to not even communicate with unbelieving family members by email resulted in a total cutting off. I miss both my mother and my sister, but my emotional and energetic investment has been, for a long time now, in my immediate family.

At the time we began to be *totally* shunned, our children were leaving home to begin their independent lives, but they still lived in the same general area, allowing for frequent visits back and forth. Terry was active with his career and I continued my practice as a psychotherapist in Montreal for twenty years. Life was good.

Having been finally able to get, use and enjoy the education I should have obtained as a young person, I decided in this later period of my life to apply to enter a doctoral program. I was accepted into the program and began to work out the details of my doctoral (Ph.D.) thesis. At the same time, my eldest daughter had her second child and my husband and I bought our dream property nestled between a mountain and a river. Wanting to spend time with my children and two grandchildren and to enjoy our new woodland property, I changed my mind and decided to withdraw from the doctoral program. A doctorate was not really essential to anything that mattered in my life and would have been nothing more than a feather in my cap - and perhaps a little "*So there!*" statement to the Watchtower Society. But at that point in my life, I didn't need the "*So there!*" statement to them anymore. I was free to continue my formal education, or not. I chose not. I did not need a Ph.D. to attract psychotherapy clients. I had no intention of applying to teach in a university, so did not need a Ph.D. for that. Freedom means you can say "*yes*" or you can say "*no*". It is wonderful to live your life without the feeling you have to justify every inclination or action with a Bible verse.

Besides enjoying gardening on our property, I have taken up photography, learned how to use Lightroom and Photoshop, and make digital photo-art and digital textures using my photographs. My husband converted a part of our garage into an art studio where I have large counters and easels for my art projects - mainly painting abstract acrylics on large canvases. It's sheer delight to be able to play with form, colour and light. There would have been no time for, or appreciation of, the need for creative expression if I were still a Jehovah's Witness. What discoveries I would have missed!

Our home is situated on a unique property that is named on maps of the area as a private park and bird sanctuary. A man who, apart from his career was also a stone mason, purchased acres of orchards here back in the nineteen-fifties. He manicured the hills and dales of the acreage around a babbling brook, building stone walls to support the terraced hills, stone bridges (some large, some small) here and there over the brook, stone arches and even stone support walls down the sides of the brook - truly magnificent work that accentuated and enhanced all the natural beauty. He gave parcels of his manicured parkland to his sons and they built their own homes here and there on the acres of land. Eventually one of those sons decided to move and sold his home to us. What luck!

Start seeing everything as God, but keep it a secret. ~Hafez

We had only been living on the property for a few days when one of the 'stone-mason's' sons, who resides in another section of the park, came to our door in a neighbourly gesture of welcome. After a friendly discussion, as he departed he said the strangest thing: "*Welcome to the kingdom!*" He was of course referring to his father's park as "*the kingdom*", but the irony of the remark was not lost on me. For half of our lives we had been working toward the establishment of God's *Kingdom*, hoping we would live in paradise under His theocratic *kingdom* rule ... and now so many years away from that preaching work and the corporation that drove it ... someone welcomes us to our new home in "*the kingdom*". How ironic and amusing! And, truth be told, it *is* our little kingdom. There are no rules or expectations in this kingdom except to be kind, loving, responsible human beings and to relax and enjoy oneself! Yes, we survived the end ... of life in a cult ... and were now enjoying life in 'paradise'. We sometimes refer to our home as "*Come-a-lot*" ... because all our children and grandchildren do!

Another day soon after our move here, I saw a man and woman walking up our driveway and as a joke I called out to Terry, "*Here come the Jehovah's Witnesses!*" He laughed and answered the door. It turned out to be another neighbouring couple wanting to welcome us to the cul-de-sac. They were sweet and even presented us with venison steaks from their freezer. When they left, Terry said something to the effect that I should have known they couldn't have been JWs because they weren't carrying any book bags! But you know ... I think I could spot a Jehovah's Witness anywhere ... I have well-honed, sensitive JW radar!

As the weeks went by, we began to notice that this couple had a similar schedule to the one we had when we were Jehovah's Witnesses - and - when they went out Saturday mornings and Sunday afternoons the brother always wore a suit and tie and ... carried a book bag. Dead giveaway. Yes, that welcoming neighbour couple were (are) Jehovah's Witnesses.

Word must have since got to them that we are 'defectors', for while they are always cordial, they have not made any more personal visits to our door, or gifts from their freezer. All that to say ... you can never really get away from them! JWs are sprinkled here, there and everywhere, and that is just fine because they are generally good people and usually make fine neighbours. Late one Sunday afternoon as Terry and I sat on a stone patio overlooking the brook and enjoying the sunshine, these neighbours drove by and waved. We waved back and then smiled at each other, knowing they were on their way to the Kingdom Hall. "*Woo-hoo*" I said, "*We're free!*". Terry said, "*I'll raise a glass to that!*"

Perhaps you are wondering if either my husband or I have joined any other religion, or if we now believe in Jehovah or any other god. Neither of us has any inclination to join an organized religion. We both feel we have given enough of our lives in the service of man-made religion and have no intention of enlisting, so to speak, a second time.

Speaking for myself, my relationship to, and belief in a god has evolved over the years since leaving the cult. When first out, I think I still believed in Jehovah and would even find myself praying to him for guidance on occasion. But as I was able to release all the old indoctrination - as I reclaimed my true self and matured - as I was able to look at the world and at history without the interfering lens of the Watchtower dogma - I began to be unsure about the existence of a supreme being in the heavens, especially a male, father figure of a god who needs to be worshipped, needs his followers to be obedient, and needs to punish them if they are not. All of that projects too many human qualities on a god for me. Thomas Merton says, "*Our idea of God tells us more about ourselves than about Him.*"

If I was going to worship a god, I did not want him to be like a grumpy, hard to please, vindictive next door neighbour. God, as most Christians see him, seems to be a projection of male qualities and desires (fatherly, righteous, demanding, protective, judgmental, domineering, exclusive, all-knowing, punitive, etc.) onto a heavenly symbol of omniscience and ultimate power. It's a source of comfort for humans to believe there's someone up there, like them, but almighty and everlasting, who knows them personally, cares for them, and will reward them for good behavior and punish others for their bad behavior. It does seem more like god made in the image of man than the other way around. I agree with Albert Einstein who said, "*I cannot imagine a God who rewards and punishes the objects of his creation, whose purposes are modeled after our own – a God, in short, who is but a reflection of human frailty.*"

A lot of wishful thinking can be found in humanity's projected images of God. I knew I did not believe in a Christian form of God, but I had not yet figured out exactly what I did believe. It took time to gather the experiences, information, and insights I needed to formulate my new, independent world view.

> *I looked in temples, churches, and mosques.*
> *But I found the Divine within my own heart.*
> ~Rumi

Most of the time, I simply said I was agnostic and did not believe in a personal god who took note of what I did or didn't do, or a god who would intervene in my life because of a prayer or a good work, or a god who would intervene on a global scale to change things on this little planet.

I now believe that we are all aspects of universal consciousness and that universal consciousness itself is the source of everything. Again I turn to Albert Einstein. He said, "*If there is any religion that could respond to the needs of modern science, it would be Buddhism.*" Some Eastern philosophies such as Buddhism, Taoism and Advaita contain very sophisticated, psychological prescriptions for living an awakened life, while not espousing the need to worship a god. In recognizing universal consciousness as the source of everything, there is no god to look to for reward or redemption. There is no need to worship anything. There is no god deciding who is wicked and who is not. There are no rewards or punishments. There is nothing to join. There are no churches to attend. There is no one to convert. There is no one asking for your allegiance or your money. There is just the free, awakened knowing of consciousness and all the ways it manifests itself as life in the universe. So pure. So simple. This way of viewing life and living life resonates with every cell of my being.

And still, after all this time, the Sun has never said to the Earth, "You owe me."
Look what happens with love like that. It lights up the sky.
~Rumi

The Dalai Lama said "*My religion is kindness*" and that sounds right to me. While I feel no need to be part of any formal religion I understand there are those who do. We must each find our own way and lead our individual, independent lives as we see fit. I have provided the above information about my current world view, not to try and convince you to my way of thinking, but because I know that once we leave the Jehovah's Witnesses we are all a bit curious about the paths other ex-Witnesses take. There are many paths and I am not promoting mine. It's wonderful to have options and no covert (or convert) agenda! That's what "*Fading Out of the JW Cult*" and being free is all about.

Why are you knocking at every other door?
Go, knock at the door of your own heart.
~Rumi

And now that this memoir draws to its close, I will redirect all this thinking and reminiscing about, and analysis of the past, back to awareness of and engagement with the present moment in whatever way it offers itself. It is in the present moment that all healing and creativity take place. Living mindfully fosters present moment awareness and, with time, helps past wounds heal. The scars from my old wounds may still be there and may even be activated from time to time, but they no longer govern my life.

Mindful present moment awareness is one of the best ways of living in the world and certainly a way of being that anyone working to heal from captivity in a cult would do well to embrace. Recent research studies confirm the value of mindful living in recovery from trauma.

You do not need to know precisely what is happening,
or exactly where it is all going,
What you need is to recognize the possibilities and challenges
offered by the present moment, and to embrace them with
courage, faith and hope.
~Thomas Merton

Connection with the body and movement of the body are also essential to achieving the well-being and peace of mind we all desire. The practices I incorporate into my lifestyle now are many of the same ones I used to effect my spiritual, psychological, and emotional recovery from the effects of being captive to a controlling, destructive cult. Practices such as:

- mindfulness
- meditation
- guided visualization
- accepting life as it unfolds, non-resistance, letting be
- allowing emotions and feelings to move through me
- energy tapping, energy medicine
- physical activity including yoga*, tai chi, and qigong
- conscious breathing
- stillness and silence
- connection with nature

- creative expression
- tight family ties, social engagement
- expressing, as needed, to a non-judgmental person, friend, or therapist
- challenging and eliminating persistent negative thoughts
- continued research via reading or resources on the web
- healthy living habits

Most items on the above list of enriching and healing lifestyle choices were not practices I could even contemplate when I was a member of the JW cult. Many of them are disparaged by the cult in some way or other. I learned to embrace many of these practices when actively working to heal from the wounds inflicted because of enslavement to JW.ORG. Now recovered, I continue to use them for the awareness, peace and the sense of psychological and physical well-being they contribute to my everyday life.

It is my hope that sharing these recollections of thirty years in a repressive cult, my struggle to leave, and the efforts to cope, adapt, learn and heal once out, will inspire you to do what you must to take full ownership of your one and only life, or affirm what you have already done if you are fortunate enough to have made your exit. Thank you for taking your precious life energy to read this memoir about my personal odyssey - *fading out of the JW cult.*

> *Do you know what you are?*
> *You are a manuscript of a divine letter.*
> *You are a mirror reflecting a noble face.*
> *The universe is not outside of you.*
> *Look inside yourself;*
> *Everything you want,*
> *You are already that.*
> ~Rumi

Recommended Reading

Books are listed alphabetically by author, although the title of the book appears first in the list. Books with asterisks are written specifically about or for JWs. The majority of books listed below are about healing from trauma and learning to live an authentic, responsible, fulfilling life whatever your circumstances.

Healing Anxiety and Depression, 2004, Daniel G. Amen
Radical Acceptance, 2004, Tara Brach
True Refuge, 2013, Tara Brach
Living Beautifully With Uncertainty and Change, 2013, Pema Chodron
How To Meditate, 2013, Pema Chodron
When Things Fall Apart, 2000, Pema Chodron
The Places That Scare You: A Guide to Fearlessness in Difficult Times, 2002, Pema Chodron
Start Where You Are, 2001, Pema Chodron
Finding Flow, 1997, Mihaly Csikszentmihalyi
The Emotional Life of Your Brain: How Its Unique Patterns Affect the Way You Think, Feel, and Live – and How You Can Change Them, 2012, Richard Davidson
Man's Search For Meaning, 2006, Viktor E. Frankl
**In Search of Christian Freedom*, 2007, Raymond Franz
**Crisis of Conscience*, 2004, Raymond Franz
Hardwiring Happiness: The New Brain Science of Contentment, Calm, and Confidence, 2013, Rick Hanson
Combating Cult Mind Control: 25th Anniversary Edition, 2015, Steven Hassan

Conscious Living: Finding Joy in the Real World, 2001, Gay Hendricks
The True Believer, 2002 (1951), Eric Hoffer
What Matters Most, 2009, James Hollis
On This Journey We Call Our Life, 2002, James Hollis
Creating A Life, 2000, James Hollis
Swamplands of the Soul, 1996, James Hollis
Childhood Disrupted: How Your Biography Becomes Your Biology, and How You Can Heal, 2015, Donna Jackson Nakazawa
The Last Best Cure, 2013, Donna Jackson Nakazawa
Full Catastrophe Living, 2013, Jon Kabat-Zinn
Wherever You Go, There You Are, 2005, Jon Kabat-Zinn
Loving What Is: Four Questions That Can Change Your Life, 2003, Byron Katie
A Lamp in the Darkness: Illuminating the Path Through Difficult Times, 2014, Jack Kornfield
Take Back Your Life, 1994, Janja Lalich & Madeleine Tobias
How Then, Shall We Live?, 1997, Wayne Muller
Legacy of the Heart: The Spiritual Advantages of a Painful Childhood, 1993, Wayne Muller
The Book of Awakening: Having the Life You Want by Being Present to the Life You Have, 2000, Mark Nepo
Yoga for Anxiety, 2010, Mary Nurrie Stearns
Beauty: The Invisible Embrace, 2005, John O'Donohue
Dream Work, 1994, Mary Oliver
The Mindful Way Through Anxiety, 2011, Susan M. Orsillo, Lizabeth Roemer
Tapping In: A Step-By-Step Guide to Activating Your Healing Resources Through Bilateral Stimulation: 2008, Laurel Parnell
Coming Home to Who You Are, 2011, David Richo
The Five Things We Cannot Change … and the Happiness We Find by Embracing Them, 2006, David Richo
How To Be An Adult: A Handbook on Psychological and Spiritual Integration. 2002, David Richo.
Letters To A Young Poet, 1986, Rainer Maria Rilke
8 Keys To Safe Trauma Recovery, 2009, Babette Rothschild
Compassion and Self-Hate, 1975, Theodore I. Rubin, M.D.
Loving-Kindness: The Revolutionary Art of Happiness, 2002, Sharon Salzberg
The Divided Mind, 2006, John E. Sarno, M.D.

The Art of Healing: Uncovering Your Inner Wisdom and Potential for Self-Healing, 2013, Bernie Siegel, M.D.
Mindsight: The New Science of Personal Transformation, 2010, Daniel J. Siegel, M.D.
The Instinct to Heal, 2004, David Servan-Schreiber
Getting Past Your Past, 2012, Francine Shapiro
Cults in Our Midst, 2003, Margaret Thaler Singer
The Untethered Soul, 2007, Michael A. Singer
A New Earth: Awakening To Your Life's Purpose, 2008, Eckhart Tolle
The Power of Now, 2004, Eckhart Tolle
The Body Keeps the Score: Brain, Mind, and Body in the Healing of Trauma, 2014, Bessel van der Kolk
Learning to Breathe: My Yearlong Quest to Bring Calm to My Life, 2011, Priscilla Warner
*Exiting the JW Cult: A Healing Handbook, 2015, Bonnie Zieman

WHAT PEOPLE ARE SAYING ABOUT:

EXiting the JW Cult:
A Healing Handbook
For Current & Former Jehovah's Witnesses

"All my life I have rested all my faith, dreams, thoughts, you name it, on the Watchtower Society. I am a 45 year old man. Just left 9 months ago. Stopped all Wt. activity 2 months back. Just about had a nervous breakdown. For two months I cried everyday at least once, like a child who's "Mother" abandoned him when I discovered all the lies, cover- ups, scandals. I loved my life as a witness. I was a zealous unstoppable "Jehu". But that dream ended in an instant of time. The worst nightmare of any witness came true. The "apostates" were right all along! As a suggestion, I believe that these 4 books should be sold as a rescue kit for ex-JW's: Crisis of Conscience, In Search of Christian Freedom, Combatting Cult Mind Control, and this MOST excellent book!!!! I suggest reading these books in this order. There is no book that can help you get on with your life quite like this book. Written by someone who was truly involved with the Watchtower and now a professional in psychology . This book gives practical, professional advice on how to deal with the psychopathic residue of this most deceptive cult. Escape the childlike behavior of having to answer to "Mother". Stand proud and feel good about your independence . Having been a totally indoctrinated "true believer", I am critical about many books. Some seem empty and repetitive about escaping the Watchtower. This is not like that. It has substance you can dig into. Do not waste time. Hit the purchase button NOW!"

"... I have just finished reading your book Exiting the JW Cult ...I am out ... your book has helped me immensely to stop licking my wounds and let them heal! I just can't say enough good about it as it has become my manual for life."

" I am really enjoying your book. It is helping tremendously in my healing and recovery ... Unlike most books that ex-Jehovah's Witnesses have written, this book helps to discover why we feel the way we do, why we do certain things, and how we react to situations based on the cult thinking that was engrained in us. Sometimes we don't even realize how much the cult has affected us. It's really a great book in the healing process and very helpful in moving past and moving forward after leaving the Jehovah's Witness cult/religion."

"Just wanted to say I am half way through your book and I absolutely love it...This book has been an amazing tool in my journey of healing ... I own a large pile of ex dub books. The two that have had the most profound effect on me are Crisis of Conscience and this healing handbook."

"In my opinion, Bonnie has written a must-read, classic, recovery book for all ex-JWs and JWs who want to leave ... this book is definitely a first for ex-JWs, and it is written so well. Wish my sister could have read it when she left the Watchtower in the mid-90s. I think she would be alive today if she had ... Bonnie's book is the next best thing to having your own personal therapist."

"...I really love this book. I have read other books on this topic but in terms of actual techniques for healing, this is the best ... Thank you, thank you, thank you for writing this book!"

"The BEST book, I've read so far by Ex-JWs!! She KNOWS her healing information! So grateful for finding this book!!!"

"Having been born and raised in a devout JW family, and having married into an equally devout JW family, I began discerning distinctions *between Bible teachings and certain Watchtower teachings by the time I turned 30. That is when I began struggling with intense feelings of guilt, although I had not adopted a practice or lifestyle for which one could be disfellowshipped from one's congregation. By the time I turned 60, I realized I could no longer accept, support or recommend the JW religion, yet I was not free to pursue Christian fellowship outside the JW religion without dire consequences; therefore, I finally disassociated from JWs, yet my feelings of guilt only intensified. Psychotherapist Bonnie Zieman helped me identify two likely sources of the guilt which has plagued me for more than 30 years. EXISTENTIAL GUILT results from denying one's true self, especially when one fails to meet one's true potential, a feeling with which many JWs can identify. NEUROTIC GUILT comes from an imagined transgression such as changing one's mind on religious matters and leaving one's religion, a feeling with which most ex-JWs can identify. While existential guilt can serve as a healthy guide back to one's true self, neurotic guilt is unhealthy and damaging and is the type of guilt placed on doubting JWs by the Watchtower. If one does not understand the difference between the positive and negative types of guilt, the punitive part of one's mind (called the Superego) assumes one has sinned and deserves punishment, and one can end up unknowingly creating forms of self-punishment (e.g. depression, failures, accidents, chronic pain, illnesses, chronic anxiety, self-sabotage, etc.) Changing one's mind and leaving the Watchtower organization is not a sin, and one doing so certainly deserves no punishment! This is what I learned from Bonnie Zieman's wonderful book, and Bonnie provides many practical suggestions on how to rid oneself of such damaging guilt so that one can enjoy a happy and fulfilling life outside of the Watchtower Society. Thank you, Bonnie Zieman!"*

About the Author

Former Jehovah's Witness Bonnie Zieman was born into the religion, married an elder, and served as a special pioneer before fading out. She went on to create a successful personal and professional life outside the cult. She holds a master's degree in education, four years' of training in gestalt and psychosynthesis psychotherapy, and specialty training in both levels of EMDR (eye movement desensitization and reprocessing therapy). Now retired, she is the author of two books offering helpful insights into the experience of leaving the all-consuming organization of Jehovah's Witness: *Exiting the JW Cult: A Healing Handbook* and *Fading Out of the JW Cult: A Memoir*. Zieman lives near Montreal in the province of Quebec, Canada with her husband. They enjoy life free from all the information, behavior and mind control they were subjected to for so many years in the repressive cult. Their three adult children also enjoy fulfilling, productive lives free of JW.ORG undue influence, interference, indoctrination and exploitation. Zieman delights in visits with her children and four grandchildren, while also enjoying photography, digital design, painting abstract acrylics on large canvases, reading, writing, and gardening.

Made in the USA
Columbia, SC
09 November 2020